ON THE MYSTICAL LIFE
VOLUME 3

ST VLADIMIR'S SEMINARY PRESS
Popular Patristics Series
Number 16

The Popular Patristics Series published by St Vladimir's Seminary Press provides readable and accurate translations of a wide range of early Christian literature to a wide audience—students of Christian history to lay Christians reading for spiritual benefit. Recognized scholars in their fields provide short but comprehensive and clear introductions to the material. The texts include classics of Christian literature, thematic volumes, collections of homilies, letters on spiritual counsel, and poetical works from a variety of geographical contexts and historical backgrounds. The mission of the series is to mine the riches of the early Church and to make these treasures available to all.

Series Editor
BOGDAN BUCUR

Associate Editor
IGNATIUS GREEN

* * *

Series Editor
1999–2020
JOHN BEHR

On the *Mystical Life*

THE ETHICAL DISCOURSES
VOLUME THREE: *Life, Times, and Theology*

St Symeon the New Theologian

written, translated, and edited by
ALEXANDER GOLITZIN

ST VLADIMIR'S SEMINARY PRESS
CRESTWOOD, NEW YORK

LIBRARY OF CONGRESS CATALOGING-IN-PUBLICATION DATA

Symeon the New Theologian, Saint, 949-1022
   On the mystical life: the ethical discourses / St. Symeon the New
   Theologian; translated from the Greek and introduced by Alexander
   Golitzin.
      p. cm.
   Includes bibliographical references and indexes.
   Contents: vol. 3 (alk paper)
      1. Spiritual Life—Orthodox Eastern Church—Early works to 1800. 2.
   Monastic and religious life—Early works to 1800. 3. Mysticism—Orthodox
   Eastern Church—Orthodox Eastern Church. 4. Orthodox Eastern
   Church—Doctrines—Early works to 1800. I. Golitzin, Alexander. II. Title.
   BX382.S96   1995   95-36925
   248.4'819—dc20   CIP

translation copyright © 1997

by

ST VLADIMIR'S SEMINARY PRESS
575 Scarsdale Road, Crestwood, NY 10707
1-800-204-2665 • www.svots.edu

First printed in 1997

ISBN 0-88141-144-2
ISBN 978-0-88141-144-7
ISSN 1555-5755

PRINTED IN THE UNITED STATES OF AMERICA

TABLE OF CONTENTS

INTRODUCTION

In the introduction which follows we shall try to provide something of the context in which St Symeon lived and wrote in order to show how and in what ways he was saying nothing new in a new way, i.e., how he was fully within the continuum of Orthodox patristic thought and at the same time was fully deserving of his title, "the new theologian."

1. The New Theologian was probably not intended as a compliment. Newness or innovation in Byzantine theology was an attribute normally associated with heretics, and it therefore seems likely that this sobriquet was originally given Symeon by his enemies[1]—of whom more below. If so, it is also true that his supporters saw the phrase as affirming a quality in their master which they welcomed as positive and necessary for their times. To call someone "theologian," after all, was to give him a rare and exalted accolade. Only two others, John the Evangelist and Gregory of Nazianzus, had ever been accorded it in such a way that it became a permanent part of their names. They received it because the Greek Church felt that they had spoken with a unique authority and had become themselves sources of theology. Thus in Symeon's case, even a twentiethcentury and not uncritical Roman Catholic scholar can write of him that he "is not merely [part of] a current carrying the contributions of the past, [but] is himself a source that enriches the Christian tradition."[2]

St Symeon never writes abstractly. Theology is never theory for him. All of his commentators, ancient and modern,

---

1   B. Krivocheine, "The Writings of St Symeon the New Theologian," *OCP* 20 (1954): 326.

2   Jean Darrouzès, "Introduction," *SC* 51, 36.

would agree with the observation that even in "his rare citations...it is not the thought of the author that he is seeking, but
the echo of his inner life."[3] That inner life, moreover, is one in
which he believes he has actually received direct revelations
from Christ, has been in direct contact with Him and taken
from Him words which "are not a fictional report, but...a
conversation which actually took place."[4] He was therefore a
theologian in the literal sense of the word. He had been given
a word (logos) by and about God, and he was obliged to report
it—even, as he tells us himself, when he would have preferred
to have kept quiet about it:

> ...I would wish to be silent—
> if only I had been able to!—
> but the tremendous marvel causes my heart to beat
>   faster,
> and opens my mouth, my tainted mouth,
> and makes me, all unwilling, write and speak.[5]

"He speaks," says his earliest modern commentator, "because
he must speak—out of the depths of his own heart."[6]

It would be mistaken to see this speaking as merely the
report of a subjective, purely personal encounter with God, i.e.,
as an exercise in the expression of religious sentiment or in the
sort of spiritual autobiography familiar to the West since St
Augustine's Confessions. There are, to be sure, interesting
points of contact (though not influence) with the great bishop
of Hippo, and that in itself points to a quality of Symeon's
uniqueness in the East to which we shall return, but the point
we feel must be underlined is the authority with which he felt
he could—and must—speak to his contemporaries:

3   Ibid. 33.

4   J. Koder, "Introduction," SC 156, 79.

5   H 1.4245 (M, 12).

6   K. Holl, Enthusiasmus und Bussgewalt beim griechischen Mönchtum:
     eine Studie zum Symeon dem neuen Theologen (Leipzig, 1898), 36.

> All you men, kings and potentates, priests, bishops,
>   monks, and married layfolk,
> do not disdain to hear my voice,
> and my words that come from a miserable man,
> but open the ears of your heart to me
> and hear and understand what He says,
>   Who is God of all...[7]

Symeon, in short, is laying claim to nothing less than the authority of a biblical prophet. If his reluctance to speak in the first quotation recalls Jeremiah,[8] here, in the second, one thinks inevitably of the formula "Thus saith the Lord" so familiar from the prophetic books. Such a claim is not new in the history of Eastern monastic literature,[9] but Symeon so emphasizes it, is so stark in his insistence on the necessity of first experiencing God in order to talk about Him—"Why do I trouble to explain and interpret?" he cries at one point, "when you will not be able to understand these things unless you have comprehended them by experience"[10]—that he introduces a note into Eastern Christian literature that had not been there before and, indeed, which has never been taken up again. He is not unique in his insistence on the experience of God as true theology, nor on the one who experiences as alone meriting the title "genuine theologian,"[11] but his tone is something in fact very new and different.

7   *H* 58.2531 (M, 288).
8   See Jeremiah 20:9.
9   See, for example, Holl, 184-185, and more recently, P. Rousseau, "The Spiritual Authority of the 'Monk Bishop,'" *JTS* 22 (1971): 384, and Sebastian Brock, "Early Syrian Asceticism," *Numen* XX (1973): 18-19, for the importance of the early monks as "spirit bearers."
10   *H* 23.517-520, and also *CH* I.41, 50 (McG, 43-44).
11   "Symeon the New Theologian,"*GOTR* 19 (1974): 110, and the article on experience (*peira*) in, especially, St Maximus the Confessor by P. Miguel, "Peira: contribution a l'étude du vocabulaire de l'expérience religieuse dans l'oeuvre de Maxime le Confesseur," *SP* (1966): 351-66, and by the same author, "La conscience de la grâce selon Syméon le nouveau théologien," *Ir.* XLII (1969): 314-322.

For the modern reader Symeon is thus truly the new theologian, "the first Eastern Christian mystic who articulated in such personal disclosures his intimate, mystical experiences for a reading public."[12] Doubtless, for his disciples and successors in the Greek tradition, his newness lay rather in the fact that he was a theologian, like the Evangelist and Gregory Nazianzus, who had appeared in their own times as "a great spiritual renovator, a restorer of the lost tradition of mystical life,"[13] and a contemporary witness to the Gospel. Yet the modern reader, particularly one used to the spiritual and theological writings of the Greek fathers, must inevitably be struck by the overwhelming force with which he presents himself and dares to speak of his own experiences in the first person singular. While no Augustine, and certainly innocent of the latter's consuming interest in philosophy and its relation to Christian theology and experience, or his confidence (one which is never duplicated in the Greeks) in the mind's capacity for searching the divine mysteries,[14] Symeon nevertheless provides the unique case of a Greek Christian writer's approaching the Western father's willingness to discuss out loud his own mind and heart. There is as well another point of possible contact with Augustine in the New Theologian's approach to the mystery of the Trinity, and we shall take that up when analyzing his thought below. For now, it is enough to emphasize that his use of "I" distinguishes him sharply from both predecessors and successors. It was also, as we shall note shortly, to bring down on him loud and apparently frequent accusations of pride and delusion. The *Discourses* translated

12 G. Maloney, *The Mystic of Fire and Light: St Symeon the New Theologian* (1979), 11.

13 Krivocheine, "Writings," 324.

14 I have in mind his confidence particularly in the soul as an adequate analogy for the Trinity, see *Civ.Dei* XI.26 and other references in our note 17, page 125 below.

below often reflect the atmosphere of controversy which surrounded him throughout virtually the whole of his active life.

2. The Main Themes of Symeon's thought may be summed up under two headings: deification (*theosis*) as "tears and light," and the spiritual father. In neither case is he anything other than a uniquely personal witness to long-established elements in the Greek patristic tradition. With respect to deification, we discover a theme whose origins we can place in the New Testament,[15] and then trace throughout the succeeding centuries: in Irenaeus of Lyons,[16] in Athansius and the Cappadocians,[17] and dominating the great debates over the nature of the union of God and man in Jesus Christ which occupy the Church in the fifth through eighth centuries.[18] St Athanasius' famous dictum, "God became man that we may be made gods," may be said to have been the *leitmotif* of the five Ecumenical Councils held between Ephesus in 431 A.D. and Nicea II in 787 A.D. St Symeon is completely the product of this development. He offers us nothing new with regard to it save, typically, his altogether characteristic emphasis on it not only as an article of doctrine, but as the intimate, personal calling of every Christian. Life in God, the Resurrection and the Spirit, are held out to us here and now. He never tires of reminding his listeners that this is the meaning of the Gospel:

> Listen and understand, Fathers, the divine words,
> and you will know the union that is effected in
>   knowledge,
> and in a perceiving awareness which is absolutely both
>   experiential and visible...
> If, the God Who has created [us]...has descended so

15 For example, 2 Peter 1:4 and John 17:5 and 22-24.

16 *Adv. Haer.* V, preface (*SC* 153, 14; *ANF* I, 526).

17 For Athanasius, see *de Inc.* 54.3 (*SC* 199, 458), and among the Cappadocians, see for example Basil's *de Sp. Sanc.* I.2 and IX.23 (*SC* 17, 252 and 328).

18 See our discussion below, 141-156.

> completely
> and united Himself with His creation...
> then the creature should really be able to perceive this
>   true happening...
> But if we do not admit this, our faith is finished.[19]

and again:

> Nay, I entreat you, let us endeavor to see Him and contemplate Him even in this life. For if we are found worthy to see Him perceptibly here, we shall not die, 'death will have no dominion over us.' Let us not wait to see Him in the future, but strive to behold Him even now...[20]

The note of urgency never leaves him. Christ Jesus comes to us now, if we would have Him, to purify us with tears in and through ascetic labor, and to give Himself to us as fire. To these two marks of divine encounter, fire (or light) and tears, together with the long and ascetic and mystical tradition from which they derive, we shall return below.

The second theme which runs through Symeon's entire life and all of his works is that of the spiritual father. It is enough at this juncture to indicate his feelings on the matter by citing the following advice from his *Letter on Confession*.

> Seek out one who is...an intercessor, physician, and a good counsellor. A good counsellor, that he may propose ways of repentance which agree with good advice. A physician, that he may prescribe medicine for you that is appropriate for each of your wounds, and finally an intercessor, that he may propitiate God by standing before Him face to face and offer Him prayer and intercession on your behalf.[21]

Himself counselled, doctored, and interceded for by his own father in God, Symeon the Pious of the Studite monastery in

19 *H* 34.1528 (M, 187).

20 *C* 3.421426 (deC, 58).

21 *Letter on Confession* 7 (Holl, 117).

Constantinople (of whom more below), our Symeon felt this relationship to have been essential for his own growth into Christ, both indispensable and of lifelong efficacy. It is with this awareness that he speaks to his own monks as their spiritual father in his *Catechetical Discourses,* and to which he returns again and again throughout his other works.

St Symeon's Life and Times

Empire and Church in the Tenth-Eleventh Centuries

The dates of St Symeon's life, 949–1022,[22] correspond roughly to the long reign of the Emperor Basil II, crowned in 960 and effective ruler from 976-1025. The saint's life is thus also contemporary with the medieval peak of the Byzantine Empire's power and splendor. Already over six centuries old at the time of his birth—that is, if we date its beginnings with the conversion of Constantine in the fourth century (or, over a millenium if we take Augustus Caesar as its founder, as the Byzantines certainly did)—the empire of Constantinople, "New Rome," was a fact of life as apparently immutable as the very earth itself. Its ruler, the Roman emperor (*Basileus ton rhomaion*), was its equally unquestioned head, a fixed part of the natural order and enjoying the writ of governance from no less an authority than God Himself. Symeon shared these assumptions, and the figure of the emperor makes frequent appearances in the body of his works. The latter also often reflect the continuous and largely successful wars of reconquest which the Emperor Basil waged throughout the saint's lifetime.[23] That Symeon did not approve the glamours of court and king, felt them indeed to be a deadly peril to the soul, is

22 We are citing here the chronology worked out by Irenée Hausherr in his "Introduction" to the *Vie de Syméon le Nouveau Théologien* (Rome, 1928), lxxx-xci.

23 See, for example, *ED* IV.208-239; the preferences for soldiers in *ED* VII.133-137; and esp. *ED* X.255-273, with its recollection of revolts within the empire which Basil II was indeed obliged to fight.

equally clear from his writings,[24] but nowhere does he seem to have questioned the rightness of the empire itself. No one else did and, in any case, his eyes were fixed on a different city, another fatherland.

As any mortal must reflect the circumstances of his or her time and place, so for St Symeon, as for his contemporaries, Constantine's city lay at the very heart of the Christian world, the capital of the Christian, Roman Empire. True, that empire now spoke Greek, had done so in fact for over three hundred years, and true again that its boundaries had mightily contracted since the days of Constantine. By Symeon's time, its former territories to the south had long been in Muslim hands, while to the west, including the "elder Rome," the new states which would eventually comprise Western Europe were beginning to stir under the leadership of the Saxon successors to Charlemagne and the first, faint glimmers of a reinvigorated papacy. These two powers, Muslim south and Latin west, would eventually shipwreck the ancient empire. The latter's longterm fragility, though, could not have been foreseen in Symeon's day. Quite the contrary, after centuries of disastrous invasions following the death of Justinian in 565, the empire's sway had been steadily advancing for years before Symeon's birth, and it carried on expanding throughout his lifetime. Basil II advanced to rule over a domain which, by his death, stretched from southern Italy to the Caspian Sea, and from the northern reaches of Croatia to the coast of Lebanon.

Yet it was still fragile. The centuries of war and invasion had largely destroyed the ancient web of cities great and little which had comprised the old empire. Learning had sagged during the troubles, with resources diverted to the military and centralization encouraged. Byzantium had emerged a fortress,

---

24 See the citation on page 34, note 1 below, and vs. wealth, see *C* 9.92-116 (deC, 152-153).

in effect an enormously extended city state. The empire's resources, its sophistication, talents and power had been concentrated in one center. Thus, dominating the whole, mistress of the lands and seas around her, Constantinople was "the guarantee for imperial stability, and...the center of both secular and ecclesiastical life."[25] Save for his last few years, all of Symeon's active life was spent in the "Queen of cities," and he was far from an unknown in the chanceries of both emperor and patriarch—a fact which would have consequences for both his personal life and his writings. It might be well, therefore, to set the stage a little further with regard to the influences around him, particularly those cultural and theological attitudes and forces at work in the capital's church and society.

In the late tenth and eleventh centuries Constantinople was enjoying something of a literary revival. The peace which had settled on the empire after 843, the end to the internal quarrel of iconoclasm, had made room for a renewal of learning, a return to the study of Greek and Christian antiquity. St Photius the Great, twice patriarch in the late 800's, was the leader. Under his patronage a modest renaissance of classical learning began which was still gathering steam by Symeon's time a hundred years later, and which would reach a kind of apogee in the career of Michael Psellos (ca. 1011-081), a contemporary of Symeon's disciple and biographer, Nicetas Stethatos (d. ca. 1090). Unlike the later Renaissance in Italy and Northern Europe, however, Byzantium's ferment was in no way revolutionary or in opposition to the givens of its medieval society. No great, intellectual upheavals or stirrings marked this period as they did Western Europe's rediscovery of classical antiquity: Byzantine instincts were unfailingly conservative. Scholarship tended to produce learned antiquarians, men and women

25 J. Hussey, *Church and Learning in the Byzantine Empire: 967-1185* (Oxford, 1937), 118.

who were largely content with repeating—or at least thinking
that they were repeating—the patterns of thought and speech
laid down centuries before by the grammarians of the Hellenis-
tic Age. Of course, this conservatism also meant a formal, not
to say rigid, adherence to the formulae of Orthodoxy worked
out by the Church fathers and Ecumenical Councils. The catas-
trophes and necessary militarization of society compelled by
the centuries of crisis had also, perhaps inevitably, led to a
certain "provincialization" of the empire and its capital, a
fortress mentality which encouraged conservatism and looked
with instant distrust on anything that smacked of the novel.
Though their numbers were probably relatively few, the literati
or humanists of imperial society were exceedingly important,
shaping as they did the empire's intellectual and theological
culture.

The Church, too, had known something of a revival in the
century preceding St Symeon's birth. The losses inflicted on it to
the south by the advance of Islam, and to the north by the Slavic
invasions which had begun in the decades following the death of
Justinian, had lately been countered by a great missionary thrust,
one of the glories of the medieval Greek Church, which, by the
tenth century, had won back for Orthodoxy the present day
territories of Serbia and Bulgaria. The effort would be crowned in
Symeon's own lifetime by the baptism of Kievan Rus and its vast,
new lands. The same great Patriarch, St Photius, had been the
patron of this movement as well. His pupil and protege, Constantine the philosopher (St Cyril), and the latter's brother, Methodius,
had laid the intellectual and spiritual groundwork for the conversion of the Slavs via their work of translation and, in Methodius'
case, missionary labors.[26] In the sphere of liturgy, liturgical poetry, and monastic reform the monastery of St John at Studion

26 For Cyril and Methodius, see D. Obolensky, *The Byzantine Commonwealth* (London, 1971), 103-104.

in Constantinople, headed by St Theodore the Studite (d. 836) and governed afterwards by a series of able successors, had imposed its stamp on both the empire's public worship and its monastic life, in particular the great center of monasticism at Mt. Athos which was aborning during our saint's lifetime.[27] It is, then, no exaggeration to speak of a kind of "golden age" as in place during the tenth and eleventh centuries. Both empire and Church stood on the crest of what must have appeared to everyone in those times as a mighty eminence. They were complete, finished products as it were, masters of all they surveyed—or, if not masters, then certain that whatever lay outside their purview could at least be dismissed as "barbarian" and not worth the candle—and unquestioned components of a world order whose rightness and permanency no one dreamt of contesting.

Of course, they were unable to see that the crest was in fact the edge of a precipice, and that what appeared to them as bright noon would prove to have been the last clear light of a long afternoon. Twilight and dusk would follow shortly. Crusaders and Turks would together bring the night to Byzantium and the Balkans while the Tatars were extending the same favor to the Slavs of what would become Russia and Ukraine. But that is another story. For the purposes of St Symeon's life, it is sufficient here to underline the notes of triumphalism and conservatism which dominated the symphony of Church and state in the Byzantium of his day. His own melody would therefore strike many of his contemporaries as discordant, impossibly jarring, and perhaps heretical. He was faced with constant opposition. Others, however, would recognize in his song the strains of a tune that was older than Constantine's alliance of Church and state, one indeed coeval with the Chris-

27 See E. Amand de Mendieta, *Mt. Athos: The Garden of the Panagia*, trans. by Bruce, (Berlin, 1972), 63-72.

tian gospel. In the long run they proved to have had the better ear. Symeon's song would eventually outlast the Christian empire itself, and it would provide the Church with something essential for her survival in the long night which was to follow the empire's fall.

Although Symeon perhaps sang his song the best, and certainly the most strikingly, we said that he was not the first to sing it. Here another feature of Byzantine Church life comes into play: the role and influence of the monks. While they were unquestioned authorities in their respective spheres, neither the emperor nor the patriarch nor their representatives were the ones most believers in the tenth and eleventh centuries turned to for answers to the question that touched them most directly: the fate of their immortal souls. Rather, for the average believer, "it was certainly to the monastery that he looked for the solution of all his ills. After political defeat, before public discomfiture, in financial embarrassment, in search of the best confessor, at every stage of his life and in every crisis," he sought out the monks.[28] While the social role of monasteries and the monks has been noted and explored in other studies,[29] here it is important to focus momentarily on the role of monastic saints, a role which Symeon exemplified in a remarkable and lastingly fertile way.

One is used, in the cultural atmosphere of Western Europe and America, to thinking of the Christian Church as something fundamentally institutional, a structure or organization staffed by officers, such as bishops and priests, and charged with the responsibility of communicating to an essentially passive laity the supernatural gifts with which it has been endowed by God in Christ. Either that, or, as in the Protestant tradition of the United

28 Hussey, *Church*, 158.

29 Ibid. 158-200, for Byzantium. For earlier in Eastern Church history, see esp. P. Brown, *Society and the Holy in Late Antiquity* (Berkeley, 1982), 103-195, and P. Rousseau, *Ascetics, Authority and the Church* (Oxford, 1978), 18-67.

States, one may picture an association of individuals, each gifted with the presence of the Spirit, who have banded together along the lines of a purely voluntary, "covenanted" or contractual relationship with God and each other. Now while these may be caricatures of, respectively, the Roman Catholic Church since the Council of Trent and the Protestant Free Church tradition represented in contemporary America by our idea of denominations, they are still close enough to the mark to underscore a divide or chasm which has haunted the Western Church at least since the Reformation: the tension between priest and prophet, institution and charism, church and sacrament versus individual and mystic. While the Eastern Church centered in Constantinople certainly knew a tension between these poles, a tension which St Symeon's whole life serves to illustrate, it was also sufficiently balanced—or blessed, depending on how one reads history—that it never had to suffer a schism between them such as would occur in the West. Where patriarch and emperor represented one of the poles, that of hierarchy, institutional authority and the sacraments, the other pole was defended chiefly, though never exclusively, by the monks. They were, in the popular eye, the primary carriers of the Church as charismatic reality, the agents and vehicles of the Holy Spirit. From monasticism's origins in the fourth century and from its oldest texts, for example the *Life of Antony*[30] and the *Sayings of the Fathers*[31] one can trace the certain "conviction that here there were people in whom the spirit and power of the Apostles continued to live with undimmed force."[32] Noninstitutional, nonhierarchical, fundamentally a lay movement—though, as we shall see, Symeon himself was ordained

---

30 PG 26.837ff.

31 PG 65.71ff, and B. Ward's excellent translation, *The Desert Christian* (New York, 1975).

32 Holl, 184-85, echoed by Rousseau, "Spiritual Authority," 384, and Brock, 18.

and had the deepest appreciation of the sacraments—monasticism in the Eastern Church supplied an unending series of holy men and women who spoke of the things of God with personal and thus authoritative conviction, who were invested with that mantle of the prophets we noted above in Symeon. It is thus no exaggeration to say, as does Bishop Kallistos Ware, that

> There are in a sense two forms of apostolic succession in the life of the Church. First, there is the visible succession of the hierarchy, the unbroken series of bishops in different cities...Alongside this, largely hidden, existing on a "charismatic" rather than an official level, there is secondly the apostolic succession of the spiritual fathers and mothers in each generation of the Church—the succession of the saints, stretching from the apostolic age to our own day, which St Symeon the New Theologian called the "golden chain"...[33]

In light of this feature of Byzantine church life, one can understand how it was that, "in matters of individual spiritual development, emperor and secular clergy could only stand aside and share, or envy, the reverence which rich and poor alike gave to those monks whom they could recognized as holy men."[34] That this reverence was no less open to abuse than the pride of princes and prelates is equally true. We can catch a whiff of the dangers of an untrammeled charismaticism in the complaint of a learned scribe who lived in Constantinople a hundred years after Symeon: "...every disgusting and thrice-accursed wretch has only to put on a monastic habit...dress himself up to look self-effacing in an ostentatious and highly theatrical way...[and] immediately the city of Constantine showers him with honors."[35] The charlatan and false "guru" is

---

33 K.T. Ware, "Forward" to *Spiritual Direction in the Early Christian East* by Irénée Hausherr, trans. by Gythiel, (Kalamazoo, 1990), vii.

34 Hussey, 119.

35 The speaker is John Tsetses, and I am quoting from Paul Magdalinos' translation in the latter's article, "The Byzantine Holy Man in the Twelfth

the unhappily necessary obverse of the charismatic elder, a fact which has troubled the "Israel of God" from Jeremiah's plaint against false prophets[36] to the eerie figure of Rasputin, one of the darker shadows lingering over tsarist Russia. Nor, as our quotation indicates, were people unaware of the perils involved in not discerning the real from the fool's gold. Symeon himself is full of warnings against would-be counsellors and saints,[37] and both he and his own spiritual father were, it seems, themselves in turn accused of charlatanism. How and why will take us to the following section.

The Life of our holy Father, Symeon the New Theologian, Priest and abbot of the Monastery of St Mamas

This title belongs to our unique source for Symeon's life, other than the evidence provided by his own writings. The *Life* was written by the saint's disciple and spiritual child, Nicetas Stethatos,[38] who himself became a figure of considerable importance and influence. He seems to have concluded his life as abbot of the great monastery of the Studion, and as an intimate of the highest authorities in the land.[39] Much of the early part of his life was dedicated to promoting the sanctity of his spiritual father, and the *Life* of Symeon that he eventually wrote has precisely this as its goal.[40] Indeed, toward the end of the *Life*, Nicetas tells us himself that not only did Symeon designate him his literary heir shortly before his death,[41] but that some thirteen years after he

Century," in *The Byzantine Saint*, ed. by Haeckel, (London, 1981), 54.
36 Jeremiah 23:9-40.
37 Examples are many. From the *Ethical Discourses*, see I.12.81-244; IV.1864 and 719-768, together with *C* 18 and 19.
38 For Nicetas, see Hausherr, *Vie*, xxiii ff and J. Darrouzès, *Introduction*, *SC* 81, 7-24 and 33-38.
39 Darrouzès, *SC* 81, 22-24.
40 Hausherr, *Vie*, xxi ff.
41 *Vie* XIV.131132 (188-90).

had died he came to his disciple in a dream instructing him to get on with the task of editing and publishing his writings—something that Nicetas confesses he had been hesitant to do for want of confidence in his own abilities.[42] The *Life* seems to have done its job well. Some seventeen years after Nicetas had received his dream visitation, Symeon was officially recognized as a saint and his relics solemnly transferred in 1052 to the capital.[43]

Yet this triumph did not last very long. The manuscripts of Nicetas' *Life* are very few, three in all,[44] and the service he composed in honor of the New Theologian has been lost completely.[45] Moreover, we hear nothing more about Symeon for more than two centuries after Nicetas' death in the 1090's. These facts indicate that, in spite of his disciple's best efforts, the saint must have remained a very controversial figure. Two studies by Jean Gouillard in the 1970's dealing with heresy trials conducted by the patriarchal chancery, particularly two such judicial inquests in the fifty year period following Nicetas' death,[46] demonstrate rather conclusively that, although Symeon remained himself posthumously free of the direct accusation of heresy, his thinking was held in high suspicion by church authorities. To be sure, his name and characteristic emphases emerge again full force in the hesychast controversy in the fourteenth century,[47] and then again in

---

42 Ibid. XIV.137140 (200-206).

43 Hausherr, *Vie*, xv ff.

44 Ibid. xiii.

45 B. Krivocheine, *In the Light of Christ*, trans. by Gythiel (Crestwood, 1986), 391.

46 See the articles by J. Gouillard, "Constantine Chrysomallos sous le masque de Syméon le Nouveau Théologien," *Travaux et Mémoires* V (1973): 313327, and "Quatre procès de mystique à Byzance," *Revue des études byzantines* 36 (1978): 581. Note also our discussion in pp. 175 ff. below.

47 See Holl, 222-223, and, for the experience of God as light, Dom Emmanuel Lanne, "Interprétation palamite de la vision de St Benoît,"

the revival of the hesychast practice led by SS. Nicodemus and Paissy Velichkovsky in the eighteenth,[48] yet his submergence for over two hundred years in the first instance, and over two hundred more in the second, indicates that he continued to prove problematic, to say the least, for the hierarchy. Bishop Basil Krivocheine has observed that it is only due to the mercy of God that the memory and writings of one of the Church's greatest saints have been preserved for us at all.[49]

Why the opposition? Those qualities of Symeon, and of monastic tradition generally, touched on above should have given some indication. Briefly, the key to grasping both the New Theologian himself and the controversy which swirled around him in his own life and afterwards is the question of charismatic authority, its basis in the conscious experience of God, and its claims, claims which extended for the New Theologian into both the right to teach of the way to God and the right to pronounce the absolution of sins.

The Events of Symeon's Life

According to the chronology worked out by Irenée Hausherr, Symeon was born in 949 to well-to-do parents in Galatea of Paphlagonia, a province in Asia Minor where his family enjoyed the status of nobles.[50] At age ten or eleven, in 960, his parents sent him to live with his uncle who had an important position at the imperial court. There, Nicetas tells us, he acquired all the studies he would need, stopping short of the advanced curriculum which would have required him to be schooled in the literature of classical (i.e., pagan) Greece.[51] At the

Le Millénaire du Mont Athos II (Venezia, 1963), 21-47, esp. pp. 30-39.

48 For SS. Symeon and Nicodemus, see G. Bebis' "Introduction" to *Nicodemus of the Holy Mountain: A Handbook of Spiritual Counsel* (New York, 1989), 37-40.

49 Krivocheine, *Light*, 62, note 74.

50 *Vie*, xc.

51 Ibid. I.2 (24).

same time, the young man rose in court service and eventually acquired the title of *spatha cubilicarius*.[52] To this point his life had followed the more or less set pattern of provincial nobility, a stay at the capital for education and insinuation into the court via a relative with influence.[53] In his fourteenth year, however, two events of singular importance occurred. His uncle lost his important position, perhaps in connection with the loss of power by the Emperor Romanos to Nicephorus Phocas in 963. Secondly, and likely as a result of his uncle's fall, the youth was introduced to the monastery of the Studion and to the man who would shape his life thenceforward, Symeon the Pious.

Nicetas scarcely mentions it at all, but there can be little doubt that Symeon the Pious was himself a controversial figure.[54] A monk, but never ordained priest, he was nonetheless engaged in the guidance of souls both within and outside the monastery. In addition, if our Symeon's *Letter on Confession* is any indication, he also exercised the authority of absolution from sins.[55] While, as we shall see below, none of these features were peculiar or unique in the monastic tradition, other characteristic patterns of the elder Symeon's behavior did give rise to gossip and accusations. Our Symeon, in insisting on his master's victory over the lusts of the flesh in *Hymn* 15, gives a rather startling glimpse of the elder's behavior:

> The holy Symeon the Pious, the Studite,
>   was not ashamed at the limbs of any man,

---

52 For this title in Byzantium, see P.A. Yannopoulos, *La société profane dans l'empire des VIIe, VIIIe, et IXe siècles* (Louvain, 1975), 36 and 72-73. That this honor, according to Yannopoulos, was reserved for eunuchs (at least prior to the ninth century) is discussed in relation to Symeon by H.J.M. Turner, *St Symeon the New Theologian and Spiritual Fatherhood* (Leiden, 1990), 18-22.

53 See Hussey, *Church*, 105.

54 This surely underlies much of the controversy that would surround Symeon himself; see *Vie* 78ff (106ff).

55 *Letter on Confession* 14 and 15 (Holl, 124-26).

> Neither to see others naked, nor to be seen naked
> himself.
> For he possessed Christ entire, was himself altogether
> with Christ,
> And he ever saw his own limbs or those of anyone else
> As one, and all as Christ.
> And [so] he remained unmoved, both uninjured and
> dispassionate,
> As being wholly Christ himself and seeing all
> The baptized as Christ, as having been clothed with
> Christ.[56]

As several of the discourses printed below indicate, not everyone was convinced of this.[57] Neither was the elder Symeon's
unusual behavior confined to occasional nudity. He would
often leave the monastery to visit spiritual children in the city[58]
and mingle freely with "harlots and publicans and sinners"[59]
who, his disciple tells us, derived great benefit from his presence.[60] Nicetas' brief remark that the elder "feigned passion in
order to disguise his freedom from it" gives the clue to the type
of spirituality he manifested.[61] He was a "holy fool," a rare form
of asceticism, but not unknown in Byzantium and, later on, in
Russia, whose asceticism consisted precisely in being thought
bizarre, insane, and even a sinner.[62] This also explains the
frequency with which our Symeon is obliged to defend his
master. Accusation and delicious scandal were surely as much

---

56 *H* 15.207215 (AK, 180; M, 56).
57 See especially *ED* IV on *apatheia* where the New Theologian feels
    obliged to defend the possibility of the saint's liberty from the passions
    even in this life.
58 *C* 16.31-44 (deC, 199).
59 *C* 20.78-98 (deC, 232).
60 See note 5 above.
61 *Vie* 81, (110).
62 See esp. the article by I. Rosenthal-Kamarinea, "Symeon Studites, ein
    heiliger Narr," *Akten des XI internationale Byzantinischen Kongress*
    (1958), 515-520.

a part of Byzantine church life as they are in the contemporary church of, for example, Orthodox Greece. The elder Symeon's form of sanctity provided ample material for the scandalmongers, and much work for his disciple later on.

Still, the young Symeon had found the master who would guide him throughout his life. He was dissuaded from entering the monastery immediately, and instead was asked to remain in the world and study the writings of St Mark the Ascetic and Diodochus of Photiki.[63] For the next several years he continued his association with his elder while working in the city as the manager of a patrician's household. Following the counsel of his elder and of St Mark to heed his conscience above all,[64] he increased his devotions, engaging in long nightly vigils of prayer, prostrations, and tears until, sometime probably in his twenty-first year, he was vouchsafed his first vision:

> ...suddenly a flood of divine radiance appeared from above and filled all the room...He [Symeon tells the story in the third person] saw nothing but light all around him...and seemed to himself to have been turned into light.[65]

Following this remarkable grace, however, the young man suffered a lapse of several years.[66] Losing the fervor which had led to the vision and abandoning regular contact with his elder, though the rupture was never complete, he "fell into more evils than had ever before befallen me."[67] In *Hymn* 34 he accuses himself of the vilest sins:

> I have been a murderer...
> ...but the manner I leave it aside...

---

63 *Vie* 4, (16).
64 *C* 22.28-51 (deC, 244).
65 Ibid. 90-98 (deC, 245-46).
66 This lapse is omitted entirely by Nicetas.
67 *C* 22.288-289 (deC, 252).

> I have also been, alas, an adulterer in my heart
> and sodomite in deed and desire
> I have been a lecher, magician, a slayer of infants,
> swearer and perjurer, greedy
> thief, liar, shameless, grasping...
> insulting, hating my brothers....[68]

While Nicetas, in commenting on this passage, runs to the defense of his master, insists that the saint ever kept his baptism "pure and undefiled,"[69] and claims that Symeon is simply providing his monks with an example of modesty, it is still certainly the case that remarks such as these, when coupled with the unusual piety of his own spiritual father, must have provided fertile ground for whisperings and rumors against both the New Theologian and the elder Symeon. In addition, while one may indeed accept that the saint is exaggerating the sins of his youth here, it would appear equally unreasonable to deny that his life in this period was of such a kind as to bring him to the "conviction" that it "would not in the end lead to his salvation."[70] Opportunities for vice, particularly in the circles of the young and privileged, were not lacking in the great city.

The conviction arrives sometime in Symeon's twenty-ninth year. Renewing contact with his elder, he travels with the latter's permission to tidy up his family affairs before entering the monastery. While there, he reads and is impressed by the *Ladder* of John of Sinai, gives himself over to austerities, and fends off the pleas of his aged father to abandon his vocation. Returning to the capital, he enters the Studion—and remains there less than a year. Initially admitted by the Abbot Peter and given to the care of Symeon the Pious, under whose tutelage

---

68 *H* 24.71-79 (M, 127).

69 See the *scholion* quoted by Darrouzès, Ibid. 233, note 1.

70 Turner, *Spiritual Fatherhood*, 29; but see also V.C. Christopherides, *He Pneumatike Patrotes kata Symeon ton neon theologon* (Thessalonica, 1977), 72-73 and note 46, page 73.

he takes on a rigorous ascetic program and experiences another vision of light,[71] the close relationship between the elder and his disciple seems to have troubled the other monks and the abbot himself, probably because they felt that the special relationship controverted the monastery's chain of command.[72] Symeon, as he will throughout his life, refuses to be separated from his elder and is asked to leave as a result. The elder sees subsequently to his incorporation as a novice into the monastery of St Mamas and, with the permission of the latter's aging abbot, continues his supervision of the young man and tonsures him monk a little later, giving him his own monastic name. With the death of the old abbot of St Mamas two years later, in 980, the young Symeon is elected his successor and ordained to the priesthood,[73] an office which he held in the greatest reverence for the rest of his life.[74] He still remains under the direction of his elder until the latter dies in 986 or 987. His *Catechetical Discourses* to his monks are marked by frequent references to his spiritual father's precepts.[75] In addition, shortly after the elder's death, Symeon composes the latter's *Life* (since lost), and begins celebrating a yearly feast in his honor complete with an icon of him and liturgical hymns celebrating him as a saint.[76] This will later provide his enemies with the ammunition they require.

Symeon is abbot of St Mamas for twenty-five years, from 980 to 1005. It would not be unfair to say that his tenure had mixed results. On the one hand, he proved an active and able administrator, once again giving the lie to the false, but frequent, assumption that the mystic is invariably incompetent in

71 *Vie* 10-19, (18-28); see also *C* 16 and *ED* IV.
72 See Turner, *Spiritual Fatherhood*, esp. 29-30 and 55.
73 *Vie* 22-33, (32-40).
74 Ibid. 34-35, (46-48).
75 Eg., *C* 16.45-70 (deC, 199-200).
76 *Vie* 72, (98).

worldly matters—the opposite, in fact, seems more usually to
be the case. He took a monastery that Nicetas describes as a
"desert" at his arrival, and built it up into a relatively large and
well-maintained community.[77] He also drew to himself disciples of outstanding virtue and ability. To one of them,
Arsenius, he would give charge of the community on his
retirement. To another, Nicetas, later on he found it possible to
entrust—not mistakenly—the serious and demanding task of
editing his writings.[78] People came to see him for counsel from
outside the strictly monastic ranks. He seems, in fact, to have
been loved by many lay people. A Western bishop seeking
penance for an accidental homicide is directed to Symeon by
no less than the Patriarch himself, and indeed finds his peace
under the saint's direction and is tonsured a member of the
community.[79] Clearly Symeon had a considerable reputation
and following. It would serve him well in his later difficulties.

On the other hand, there were difficulties. The Byzantine
monastery was inevitably a "mixed bag." If monasticism was
the primary carrier of a charismatic tradition going back to
Antony and the Desert Fathers—and beyond—it was also a
kind of catch-all for the bruised, the disappointed, the rural and
urban poor looking for a better way of life together with an
upgrade in social standing, and for the politically marginal,
losers in the perilous enterprise of Byzantine politics. Remark-
ing on the last, Professor Hussey writes:

> ...Faced with defeat and possibly with death...one political
> figure after another appears in the records of his time only
> to be dismissed with the all too familiar words "he became
> a monk"...the usual imperial means of housing enemies
> was confinement within the walls of a monastery.[80]

77 Ibid. 34-35, (46-48).

78 Ibid. 45-51, (58-66).

79 Ibid. 52-58, (68-76).

80 Hussey, *Church and Learning*, 162-163.

Still others were "birds of passage who...flitted from the secular
to the monastic...[with the] inability or refusal to recognize the
real purport of a monk's life."[81] While there is no mention of
political losers within the company of St Mamas, it is a safe
assumption that the community embraced a pretty fair sample
of the other, less certain vocations mentioned.

Our saint, however, was not of a temperament that went
easily with half-measures. His *Catechetical Discourses*, given
to his monks during the morning services,[82] provide ample
witness to the power and absolute nature of the monastic
calling. While they are unquestionably thrilling, and comprise
a wonderful testimony to Symeon's burning concern for the
souls placed in his charge,[83] they must as certainly have
seemed daunting indeed to monks of the more tepid variety,
unused to discipline and unready to accede to the demands he
placed upon them. Symeon as abbot, the "crazy zealot" and
"brother-loving poor man" desperately eager to share the
wealth he had discovered in Christ[84] and determined that his
charges understand, would not bend: "When he himself was
confronted by many who were more or less incapable of
sharing his ideals, his reaction was simply to reiterate them."[85]
The result was rebellion. Sometime in the mid-990's after
fifteen or so years as abbot, thirty of the monks set upon him
during one of his morning lectures. Nicetas says they were
prevented from tearing him to pieces with their bare hands only
by his calm demeanor and a "power from above."[86] The attack

81 Ibid.
82 See *Vie* 38, (50).
83 See esp. his charge to his successor, Arsenius, which comprises the
    whole of *C* 18.
84 For "brother-loving poor man," see C 34.36ff, and for "crazy zealot,"
    C 21.39-40. For comment, see Krivocheine, *Light,* 15-42, with his article,
    "The Most Enthusiastic Zealot," *Ostkirchliche Studien* IV (155): 108-28.
85 Turner, *Spiritual Fatherhood*, 224.
86 *Vie* 38-39, (50-52).

broke up and the dissidents ran off instead to set their complaint before the Patriarch. He gave them little joy, but instead packed them off into exile. The saint, however, went in search of his lost sheep and, if Nicetas is to be believed, succeeded in bringing them back into the fold.[87] There were sound reasons for this return other than Symeon's genuine pastoral concern. The rebels were unlikely to have found the security they had known inside the monastery once outside its walls. Nicetas tells us Symeon found many of them wandering "here and there," homeless in the great city.[88] In any event, the episode demonstrated that not all could or would see things their abbot's way, and he must have been obliged to deal with a still—if hiddenly—truculent and resentful minority throughout the remainder of his abbacy.

The latter would come to end because of another and more serious dispute involving the highest authorities in the Byzantine Church and concluding with St Symeon's exile from the city—at first compelled, and later voluntary—for the last seventeen years of his life. The argument turned, at least ostensibly, around his veneration of his beloved spiritual father. Deeper issues were doubtless involved, and they shall be taken up presently, but for now the facts of the matter so far as they can be distinguished are as follows: an initial disagreement over a question of trinitarian theology with a high church official led the latter into a full-fledged and long-fought campaign against the public cult of Symeon the Pious at St Mamas and, as a result of his refusal to comply with the eventual Judgment of the patriarchal court against him, our Symeon's enforced exile.[89]

The villain of the piece, at least painted thus and in the blackest dye by Nicetas, was a certain Stephen, sometime

---

87 Ibid. 40-41, (52-54).

88 Ibid. 54; see also Hussey, *Church and Learning*, 178-79.

89 Ibid. 72-79, (98-136).

metropolitan of Nicomedia, who had resigned his episcopacy
in order to serve as *synkellos* (chancellor) in the patriar-
chate—doubtless a move up in the ecclesiastical world. Although Nicetas portrays him as a distillate of malice and envy
compounded by choler, the reality was surely somewhat less
horrific. What little is known of him outside Nicetas' *Life*, a
passing mention of him as diplomat and one surviving letter,[90]
when coupled with Nicetas' own admission that he was a man
of superior attainments "in both learning and knowledge,"
close "to both patriarch and emperor" and capable of sound
advice while enjoying a great "reputation for science,"[91] indicates that here was an example of that learned elite we noted
above, one of the cream of the Byzantine humanist revival
underway since the time of St Photius. In Stephen's reaction to
Symeon, which Nicetas again rather overplays as a simple
confrontation between worldly wisdom and the unlettered illumination of the Holy Spirit, we can perhaps discover a kind of
distillate of the tension in Eastern Church life between hierarchical and charismatic authority. Additionally, in the specific
context of the early eleventh century, it indicates the growing
distrust between the advocates of secular learning and canonical rule, on the one hand, and monastic suspicion of the first
and freedom regarding the second, on the other, which would
grow throughout the century and result, in the twelfth and
thirteenth centuries, in the apparent victory of such men as
Stephen, together with the effective ostracism and condemnation of those following Symeon's lead.[92]

---

90 See *PG* 122.153AB, and, for Stephen's surviving letter, M.P. Vinson's
    The Correspondence of Leo, Metropolitan of Synada and Syncellus
    (Washington, D.C., 1985), 56.

91 *Vie* 74, (100). Thus Hausherr, lxvi, is inclined to take Nicetas' denun-
    ciations with a pinch of salt.

92 See the articles by Gouillard and Magdalinos cited above, as well as pp.
    175ff below.

However, this struggle was only in its opening phase in the New Theologian's day and, in his own time at least, he would emerge the victor—though not without initial reverses. The quarrel began in 1003 with an apparently innocent request by Stephen, meeting Symeon on the steps of the patriarchal chancery, for a clarification of his teaching on the meaning of the union between the Persons of the Trinity, specifically whether the Three were to be distinguished in thought (*epinoiai*) or in fact (*pragmati*). Symeon agrees modestly to the request and promises a letter. The two part with the sort of smiling pleasantries reserved, especially in the East, for cultivated adversaries.[93] Of course, the question was a loaded one. Symeon could have easily fallen into either tritheism or modalism and so open himself up to ecclesiastical censure. While, as we shall see below, there may have been reasons for Stephen's having doubts as to his orthodoxy on the Trinity, it is hard not to agree with Nicetas in seeing this request as the deliberate attempt of a learned theologian, concerned with due order in the Church, to bring an already famous charismatic down a peg or two in popular esteem by showing him up publicly as either a heretic or, at the least, as a theological illiterate.

If it was such a ploy, it failed to work. Stephen must have been disappointed by the answer he did get. He was certainly infuriated. Taking Symeon's *Hymn* 21 as his promised letter to the chancellor,[94] we find it beginning with the insulting inscription, "To a Monk," referring to Stephen's reversion to monastic status on leaving the episcopate. It was technically correct, but intentionally not very diplomatic. The letter then moves quickly to discern the trap in the question and to render it harmless:

Even if He [the Son] is separated [from the Father], yet

---

93 *Vie* 75-76, (102-104). The German expression, *scheissfreundlich*, springs to mind here.

94 See the comment by Neyrand in *H* 21, (130-131, note 1).

it is not by nature, but
rather by His Hypostasis, or thus by His Person
    [*prosopon*],
for to say "in fact," that belongs to the impious and
    atheists,
and "by reason," belongs to those who are wholly
    plunged into darkness...[95]

Both alternatives are specifically identified as heretical:

For whether they separate the Word by a mental
    distinction or by a real one, from both sides, they
foolishly err and fall into heresy.
For 'in fact' is to cut the Word off,
While 'in thought' is to confuse Him [with the Father]
    so as no longer to distinguish Him.[96]

Neither is Symeon content merely to protect himself. In his eyes, Stephen is treading on ground where he does not belong. To speak of divine things is reserved uniquely for those who have known God. Thus his letter moves from defense to attack:

How do you not shudder, tell me, to speak of God?
How dare you, you who are completely flesh
and have not become Spirit, like [St] Paul,
how dare you to philosophize or speak about the Spirit?[97]
...now leave God alone!
For fear that the whole creation tremble and fall,
and annihilate your thick flesh
and shatter your carnal soul...[98]

The proper response to the mysteries of God for people like the chancellor is not arrogant presumption, but humility and mortification. Then only, Symeon tells his interlocutor in the first of his *Theological Discourses*, may he "speak of divine and

95 *H* 21.303 (M, 95).
96 Ibid. 307-311 (M, 102).
97 Ibid. 173-176 (M, 99).
98 Ibid. 450-453 (M, 105).

human things and I, too, shall recognize the power of your words."[99]

The emphasis on experience as *sine qua non* of theology echoes throughout the *Discourses* printed below, and indeed all of Symeon's works. It could not have failed in this instance to make an avowed enemy of Stephen. He was doubtless angered by the personal attack and, to allow him some credit, disturbed by the extent to which Symeon pushed his claims to charismatic authority.[100] If, as Hausherr conjections,[101] Stephen was involved in the contemporary effort to sort out the canonical procedures for canonization, the chancellor's change in attack from theological questions to those which we might call "due process" makes very good sense. Of note, too, is the fact that, even in an atmosphere where heresy trials involving alleged Manicheanism and Messalianism[102] were increasingly common, Symeon "was never, or almost never, accused of heresy, even less of Messalianism or any other known heresy."[103] Rather the "church hierarchy," motivated by the chan-

---

99 *TD* I.301-303 (McG, 117).

100 Hausherr, *Vie*, lxvii-lxxx (esp. lxxix-lxxx), rather inclines to Stephen's side here. See also Darrouzès, *SC* 81, 33. Both modern critics share with the chancellor a certain concern to keep charismatic authority within definite bounds.

101 Hausherr, lv.

102 See the articles by Gouillard cited above, together with H.J.M. Turner, "St Symeon the New Theologian and Dualist Heresies," *SVTQ* 32 (1988): 359-66, and Milan Loos, *Dualist Heresy in the Middle Ages* (Prague, 1972), 31-102, esp. 81-98.

103 Krivocheine, *Light*, 62. "Messalianism" (Greek "Euchites") derives from the Syriac word for prayer. This "heresy," denounced by writers from Ephiphanius and Theodoret in the fifth century to John Damascene in the eighth, comprises one of the more confusing—and confused—subjects of modern scholarly controversy. It appears as a monastic movement (though movement may be too strong a term) in the latter part of the fourth century. In so far as it was a heresy, the latter seems to have lain in the Messalians' contention that the Holy Spirit may be known physically and that, given this experience, one would be forever free of the temptation to sin, apathes. Emphasis, it seems, was thereby placed on personal prayer

cellor, "preferred to limit the conflict to the questions regarding discipline and the troubles that tumultuous celebration of the memory of Symeon the Pious would have caused the people."[104] Thus for some six years, from 1003 to 1009, Stephen is behind an effort to discipline the abbot of St Mamas for, in effect, having canonized his spiritual father without benefit of hierarchical blessing. The issue is somewhat complicated because, if Nicetas is to be believed, the Patriarch had some years before tacitly confirmed the public veneration of the elder Symeon by congratulating the New Theologian on the hymns he had composed in his elder's honor and by sending him candles and incense for the service.[105] Stephen, however, presses for proofs of the elder's sanctity, and makes one of those unusual features of the latter's spirituality noted above to suggest that he was in fact something less than perfectly dispassionate (*apathes*).[106] Our Symeon's vigorous defense of his master's complete freedom from fleshly appetites is reported by Nicetas,[107] and it can be seen as well to underlie several of the *Discourses* printed below, especially numbers IV, V, VII, and IX.

The first phase of the battle concludes with Symeon's resignation from the office of abbot in 1005, but further sessions with the synod of the Constantinopolitan church follow over the next three years. While at first reluctant to move on the matter,

to the exclusion of the sacraments—see John Damascene, *Liber de Haeresibus* 81, ed. by Kotter, (Berlin, 1981), 42-48. In modern scholarship, as in tenth to twelfth-century Byzantium, the label "Messalian" seems often to have been pasted onto what is in fact "a great current of ancient monastic and mystic spirituality, perfectly Orthodox in its origins." Krivocheine, 31-32, note 19. For further discussion and reference to scholarly literature, see our note 81, page 72 below.

104 Krivocheine, *Light*, 62.
105 *Vie* 73, (100).
106 Ibid. 79ff, (108ff).
107 Ibid. 83-91, (112-124).

perhaps for fear of imperial intervention on the New Theologian's behalf (he seems to have had powerful friends at court), the Patriarch finally orders the removal and destruction of the icons of Symeon the Pious[108] and the cessation of his liturgical commemoration. Our Symeon refuses to obey. In consequence he is sentenced in January 1009 to exile from the capital.

Nicetas paints a mournful picture of the saint abandoned by all and dropped ashore to sit helpless in the ruins of a small monastery—St Macrina's—on the far side of the Bosphorus while his ruthless enemies, Stephen in particular, ransack the few possessions left behind at St Mamas.[109] The reality must have been much less bleak. Symeon's powerful friends are at work almost immediately extending him their sympathy and help. At the same time, they are threatening the Patriarch with imperial action on their elder's behalf.[110] He is given charge of the ruined monastery together, we may be sure, with money to rebuild it,[111] and he does so, quickly gathering a new flock of disciples about himself in the process.[112] Faced with the threats of Symeon's friends, the Patriarch reverses himself a year or so after the exile (1010-1011), and lifts the condemnation. Even Symeon's refusal to mitigate in any way the commemoration of his spiritual father draws from the beleaguered archbishop no more than the half admiring, half rueful remark that the New Theologian is a "genuine Studite"[113]—an allusion to that monastery's (deserved) reputation for resistance in the name of theological and moral principles to misguided or

108 Ibid. 92-93, (126-128). Nicetas rather clouds the issue by comparing this disciplinary action to the violence of the Iconoclast emperors, and feels free in consequence to cite John Damascene's defense of the icons against Stephen's efforts.
109 Ibid. 94-98, (130-136).
110 *Vie* 101-102, (140-142).
111 Ibid. 100, (138).
112 Ibid. 110, (152).
113 Ibid. 103-108, (142-150).

heretical church authorities.[114] He even offers Symeon a bish-
opric by way of compensation for his injuries. The offer is
refused, but the two part on amicable terms with Symeon
having permission to live wherever he chooses. He elected to
remain in his now voluntary exile where, as Nicetas remarks,
he could rest and give himself completely to conversation with
God and, very probably, the composition of his *Hymns* and
several other works.[115]

It is during this last phase of the saint's life that Nicetas
himself comes into contact with him. The final years are
marked by quiet, the report of miracles, and a deathbed
scene—to which Nicetas was certainly an eyewitness—worthy
of the great saints of the past.[116] On March 12, 1022, having
foreseen his approaching end and made his communion, the
saint breathes his last while his monks begin singing the fu-
neral office. He was, Nicetas concludes, a man apostolic in
works and thoughts who lived in accordance with Christ and
possessed within himself the grace of the Holy Spirit.[117] His
intercessions and links with his disciples, as the concluding
sections of the *Life* seek to demonstrate, remained unbroken.[118]
In Christ, the saint had proved victorious over death.

Charismatic vs. Institutional: On Confession
and the Role of Experience

The clash between Symeon the New Theologian and Stephen
of Nicomedia was part of a larger story, "an episode in the
longstanding conflict between pneumatic monachism and hierarchical authority,"[119] which had been going on for centuries in

114 See J. Meyendorff, *Byzantine Theology* (London, 1974), 56-58.
115 *Vie* 111, (154).
116 Ibid. 113-129, (156-186).
117 Ibid. 130, (188).
118 Ibid. 131-152, (188-228).
119 Paul McGuckin, "Introduction," *Practical and Theological Chapters*

in the Christian East and which would, given a certain consensus arrived at in the fourteenth century, continue without interruption to the present day. Although the patriarchal inquiry and condemnation had been couched in such a way as to avoid raising matters of principle, the heart of the matter came down to the question of authority in the Church. By moving "precipitously" to canonize his spiritual father, Symeon was in effect claiming the right to do so on the basis of his elder's manifest sanctity, as a man whom the Holy Spirit had indwelt. He also did so on the strength of his own, often repeated assertion that he, too, had been thus blessed and so could discern rightly his master's holiness. In the fourteenth *Ethical Discourse,* for example, he states that it was through his elder's prayers that he received the Spirit:

> ...We know that the holy Symeon the pious...became such a one, and we have been confirmed in this by experience itself. For, having had our faith in him confirmed by the revelation of the Spirit within him, we hold this truth as incontestable. Yet more: the lamp of our own soul was kindled by communication from his light, as flame from one lamp to another. We preserve [that flame] unquenched, are guarded by his prayers and intercessions, whence our faith in him is watered and grows....[120]

In his *Practical and Theological Chapters* he can thus speak of the succession of saints as a continuum of light and life, using language which deliberately recalls the *Celestial Hierarchy* of Dionysius the Areopagite:

> The intelligible orders of the higher powers are illumined by God from the first order to the second, and from there to all the others in the same way until the divine light passes through them all. The saints, too, are illumined in the same way by the divine angels, and as

(Kalamazoo, 1982), 18.
120 *ED* IX.248-57.

they are bound up and joined together in the bond of the
Spirit, they become their equals and emulate them.
These saints themselves come after the saints who pre-
ceded them, and from generation to generation they join
[their predecessors] through the practice of God's commandments. Like them, they are enlightened and receive this grace of God by participation. They become
just like a golden chain with each one of them a link,
bound to all the preceding saints in faith, love, and good
works...one single chain in the one God....[121]

Here is that second line of "apostolic succession" we found
suggested by Bishop Kallistos above. The problem lay—and
lies—in the question of its overlap with the duly constituted,
visible hierarchy of Church officers, bishops and presbyters.
While Symeon's works are full of angry denunciations of
contemporary authorities, secular and sacerdotal, together with
warnings against people presuming to take on leadership
within the people of God before having received the blessing
of God, and criticism of displays of power and influence,[122] he
never doubts that the hierarchical and sacramental structures of
the Church are true and established by God. Nor was the
accusation that he was "messalian"—i.e. that he deprecated the
sacraments and held for a purely spiritual line of authority—ever advanced against him, though this does seem to have
happened posthumously and, as it were, by proxy.[123]

One place, however, where Symeon does appear clearly to
overstep the line and fall into heresy, or at least error, is in his

---

121 *CH* III.4 (McG, 72-73). See Dionysius *CH* IV.3 (*PG* 3.181A; Heil and
Ritter, 22; Luibheid, 157) and V (*PG* 3.196B; Heil and Ritter, 25;
Luibheid, 159) for the descent of illumination through the hierarchy of
angels, and *DN* III (*PG* 3.680C; Suchla, 139; Luibheid, 68) for a
suggestion, albeit in a somewhat different context, of the "chain"
imagery.

122 See esp. *ED* V.296-559, the *Letter on Confession* 13 (Holl, 123), *H*
58.25ff (M, 288ff), and *C* 18.829 (deC, 209-10).

123 Gouillard, "Quatres Procès," esp. 35-39.

remarkable *Letter on Confession.*[124] Here he specifically addresses the question whether "it is...permissible to confess one's sins to monks who are not priests" since, he notes, some say that the authority "to bind and loose has been given exclusively to the priests."[125] The answer he comes up with might surprise or even shock: "this grace is given alone to those...who have been numbered with Christ's disciples on account of their purity of life,"[126] and he concludes with:

> My child, I know that the authority to bind and loose is given by God the Father and our Lord Jesus Christ through the Holy Spirit to such people, to those who are sons by adoption and His holy servants. I was myself a disciple to such a father, one who did not have the ordination from men, but who brought me by the hand—or better, by the Spirit—into discipleship, and who commanded me...to receive the ordination from men according to the traditional order.[127]

He clearly felt that his own master, Symeon the Pious, did have the authority to pronounce forgiveness of sins even though the latter remained all his life a simple monk. Moreover, Symeon proposes a whole theory concerning the transmission of this authority which links it with personal sanctity and the experience of God. Beginning with Christ's bestowal of the authority to bind and loose on the Apostles in 20:22-23, he moves to its succession:

> ...only the bishops had that authority to bind and loose which they received in succession to the Apostles. But, when time had passed and the bishops became useless, this dread authority passed on to priests of blameless life and worthy of divine grace. Then, when the latter in their turn

124 See Holl, 289-314, on early debate over the position Symeon maintains in the *Letter*. See also J. Erickson, *The Challenge of our Past* (Crestwood, 1991), 23-38.

125 *Letter on Confession* 1.35 (Holl, 100).

126 Ibid. 13.20-21 (Holl, 124).

127 Ibid. 15.39 (Holl, 127).

had become polluted, both priests and bishops becoming like the masses with many—just as today—tripped
up by spirits of deceit and by vain and empty titles and
all perishing together, it was transferred, as we said
above, to God's elect people, I mean to the monks. It
was not that it had been taken away from the priests and
bishops, but rather that they had made themselves alien
to it...[128]

From this he concludes that ordination does not automatically
confer the worthiness to forgive sins:

Perish the thought! For these [the clergy] are allowed
only to celebrate the sacraments [*hierourgein*]—and I
think myself that even this does not apply to many of
them, lest they be burned up entirely by this service who
are themselves but straw! Rather, this grace is given
alone to as many as there are among priests and bishops
and monks who have been numbered with Christ's disciples on account of their purity of life.[129]

One source of the difficulty the modern Orthodox or Roman
Catholic may have with this series of statements—not to mention
the scholars who have written on the question in Symeon[130]—is
that the distinction between spiritual counsel and the act of
sacramental absolution had not really been made in the new
Theologian's day. In the Orthodox world, the distinction seems
to have become generally accepted only following the failed
union council with the Roman Church at Lyons in 1274. Thus,
for example, by the time of Symeon of Thessalonica in the
fifteenth century absolution has indeed become a *leitourgema*,
i.e., a specifically sacramental action celebrated by a priest.[131]

128 Ibid. 11.2-12 (Holl, 120).

129 Ibid. 13.17-21 (Holl, 124).

130 See, for example, J. van Rossum, "Priesthood and Confession in St
    Symeon the New Theologian" *SVTQ* 20 (1976): 220-28, and V.C.
    Christophorides, 56-57.

131 Holl, 329. For this shift, in part the adoption in the East of the Western

We note here that Symeon does limit such sacramental actions (*hierourgein*) to the ordained clergy in the text just cited, but the fifteenth century is, after all, four centuries later than the New Theologian. To fault him for failing to make this distinction is an anachronism.

Secondly, however, this should not obscure the fact that in Symeon's day, and from long before his time, there was a very real tension in the life of the Church over the understanding of penance and its accompanying discipline. From the time of St Cyprian of Carthage in the 250's C.E.—and, indeed, one can see the question emerging in the *Shepherd of Hermas* a century before[132]—the question of the possibility of forgiveness of mortal sin following Baptism, and who should be the agent of that forgiveness, had exercised the Christian Church. Beginning with Cyprian's *On the Lapsed*[133] through, for example, St Basil the Great's canons regarding the readmission of sinners to communion,[134] the role of the bishop in determining who would or would not be readmitted and under what conditions had been central. This culminated in the Latin Church with the Blessed Augustine's response to the Donatists: the duly ordained administer the sacraments and that administration has nothing to do with the personal worth, or lack of it, of the minister[135]—a point to which we shall return momentarily. The canonical penances administered by the bishops were

Church's notion (and list) of seven sacraments, c.f. A. De Halleux, "Confirmatio et chrisma," *Ir.* 57 (1984): 490-515, esp. 493-94.

132 See the "Introduction" to the *Shepherd* by R. Joly, *SC* 53, 22-30, and in the *Shepherd* itself, Mandate 4.3.

133 On the Lapsed 15-22, (PL 4.482A-484A), together with his Epistles 9, and 33 (PL 4.256-A259B and 325A-329A; English translation, Early Latin Theology, ed. by Greenslade, esp. 145-46).

134 See Nicodemus the Hagiorite, Pedalion, (Thessalonica, 1991, rep. of 1864 ed.), 586-649 (Eng. trans. by Cummings, *The Rudder* [Chicago, 1957], 772-86); and Holl, 225-88.

135 See his theology of baptism in Book I of *On Baptism: Against* the Donatists, *PL* 43.107-126 (English in *NPNF*, 1st Series, vol. IV, 411-24).

exacting, to say the least.[136] But, with the rise of the monastic movement, another force comes into play. In the *Sayings of the Fathers,* for example, we find specific instances of the desert elders reacting against the harsh penances imposed by church authorities. Thus:

> A brother questioned Abba Poeman saying, "I have committed a great sin and I want to do penance for three years." The old man said to him, "That is a lot." The brother said, "For one year?" The old man said again, "That is a lot." Those who were present said, "For forty days?" He said again, "That is a lot." He added, "I myself say that if a man repents with his whole heart and does not intend to commit the sin anymore, God will accept him after only three days."[137]

Note that in this passage Abba Poemen is not so much claiming the authority to forgive sins, whether by virtue of apostolic succession or of a charismatic endowment, as he is stating the conditions under which God will receive the sinner back into communion. His authority is revealed in the fact of his confidence, even against the views of his interlocutor which reflect prevailing ecclesiastical practice, that this is indeed the way that is pleasing to God: "I myself say that...God will accept him." The same attitude is reflected in an identical story involving the Abba Sisoes which concludes with the latter's firm avowal: "But I trust in God that if such a man does penance with his whole heart, God will accept him, even in three days."[138] Likewise, the Abba Lot counsels an erring brother to fast, and, "After three weeks, the old man had the certainty that God had accepted the brother's

---

136 And not only in Basil's time, as cited in note 2 above, but see as well the "moderation" of penances which Nicodemus provides in his Exomologetarion (Athens, reprint of 1868 Venice ed.), 77-91.

137 Poemen 12, *PG* 65.325A (B. Ward, *The Desert Christian*, 169). See also H. Dörries, "The Place of Confession in Ancient Monasticism," *SP* 5 (1962): 284-311, esp. 291-97.

138 Sisoes 20.400AB (Ward, 217).

repentance."[139] It is the certainty of the old men which is the badge of their authority. They have precisely that boldness (*parresia*) before God which Symeon, six hundred years later, declares essential for anyone who would say to another, "Be reconciled with God."[140]

In the six centuries between the *Sayings of the Fathers* and the *Letter on Confession* the Eastern monastic tradition provides an unbroken witness to the same basic theme, that "whoever would grapple with the most intimate affairs of another must himself have personal authority,"[141] i.e., the authority deriving at once from personal struggle with sin and from the experience of God's forgiveness and consequent familiarity with Him. That such men were to be found primarily among the monks, as opposed to the secular clergy, was simply a given. This is surely demonstrated by the fact that Symeon's remarks above on the succession of the authority to forgive sins to the monks "was never condemned by the Church...nor was it rejected by clerical opinion."[142] True, it was never officially approved, and in the century following Symeon some, such as the canonist Theodore Balsamon, would begin to draw sharp lines distinguishing spiritual counsel from the authoritative word of priestly absolution[143]—perhaps in reaction to the very phenomenon we have been discussing—yet this came much later, long years after the New Theologian's own lifetime. Even so, the matter of charismatic vs. institutional authority remained, and has continued to remain, less clear in the Greek East than in the Latin West.[144] The authoritative word of

139 Lot 2.256AB (Ward, 122).

140 *Letter on Confession* 14 (Holl, 124).

141 Holl, 331; see as well 225-330 for the demonstration of continuity in Eastern monastic literature in this regard from Antony to Symeon, and beyond.

142 Krivocheine, *Light*, 139.

143 See Holl, p. 323, and Christophorides, p. 57.

144 Very illuminating in this regard are the essays which P. Brown has

forgiveness, like the logion of the Desert Fathers,[145] is still seen by many in the Orthodox world as presupposing some personally acquired authority on the part of the one who gives it.[146]

But, before leaving the question specifically of penance, let us dwell, thirdly, on the meaning of that authoritative word for Symeon. We saw that the authority of Poemen, Sisoes and Lot derived from their insight into the nature of sin, repentance, and God's forgiveness, an insight won from their own experience of all three, and in particular of the last. They speak authoritatively of what they know, God and the workings of the human heart, and from this knowledge they prescribe the ways which the penitent must follow in order to find reconciliation. Their prescription is true and efficacious because of their experience and the discernment given as a result of it. The point lies in the word "prescription." The fathers of monasticism were revered because they had acquired knowledge of the ways of God and so could direct others along the right path. They were the true diagnosticians of spiritual maladies, the physicians of ailing souls who stood ready to provide the cure.[147] This is also Symeon's view.

collected in his *Society and the Holy in Late Antiquity* (Berkeley, 1982), 103-195, and esp. 166-195. For similar views, see J. Meyendorff, *The Byzantine Legacy in the Orthodox Church* (Crestwood, 1982), 153-165 and 197-215, as well as Rousseau, *Authority*, esp. 18-67.

145 See Dörries, "Confession," 289.

146 Thus, for example, the traditional recourse of Eastern Christians to monasteries for spiritual counsel, a preference which continues to the present day. See, for example, the recently published reminiscences of Archimandrite Cherubim, *Recollections of Mt. Athos* (Brookline, 1987), together with the same author's *Contemporary Ascetics of Mt. Athos* (Platina, 1992); Archimandrite Hierotheos Vlachos' *A Night in the Desert of the Holy Mountain* (Levadia, Greece, 1991); S. Bolshakoff's *In Search of True Wisdom* (Garden City, New York, 1979); and P. Pascal's *The Religion of the Russian People*, trans. by R. Williams (Crestwood, 1976), esp. 39-53.

147 The physician imagery for the spiritual father is deeply rooted in the ascetic and spiritual tradition. See, for example, K.T. Ware's "Forward" to *Spiritual Direction in the Early Christian East*, xii-xiii.

The spiritual father is physician, and he has come to be a doctor of souls because he knows Christ:

> Christ, the true light, when He had come and met with those who seek Him, in a way that He alone knows, gave them grace to see Himself. This is what it means to find one's own soul: to see God, and in His light to become oneself higher than all the visible creation, and to have Him inside oneself as shepherd and teacher. From Him as well, this person will know how...to bind and loose, and, as knowing truly, will worship the One Who gave this grace and Who will provide it in turn to those in need.[148]

What then is the content of this "binding and loosing?" How is one reconciled to God by the spiritual father? By "obeying" the latter's "ordinances and commandments" with all one's soul.[149] True, the role of physician does not exhaust the role of the true confessor for Symeon. The power of the elder's intercession before God on behalf of the penitent is at least of equal weight[150]—as it is, indeed, for the Desert Fathers[151]but, in both cases, the function of "binding and loosing" is not conceived of as an objective power, a capacity to command, but rather in terms of relationships. As physician and intercessor, Symeon's confessor directs healing and prescribes medication for the penitent while pleading with God on his behalf as "friend to friend."[152] There is no *ego te absolvo* in the New Theologian's thinking on this issue, no formula of sovereign command, nothing impersonal. Rather, almost everything is personal for

---

148 *Letter on Confession* 14.25 (Holl, 126). See also *Vie* 36, (48), and *C* 18.288ff (deC, 217-218) for the necessity of the abbot having this experience. Note also Symeon's recollection of his own experience and training in this vocation in *H* 30.304-352 (M, 166-167).

149 Ibid. 16 (Holl, 127).

150 Ibid. 78 (Holl, 117-118).

151 See again Lot 2, cited in note 141, page 45 above, where the elder takes on half the burden of the penitent's sin.

152 *Letter on Confession* 14 (Holl, 124).

him, and hence everything—or almost everything—depends
on the quality of the persons involved.[153]

The last remark at once takes us back to the issue with
which we began and does point out a real difficulty in
Symeon's thought. If everything is personal, and if personal
sanctity therefore is the true measure of all that which is of
God, what happens in consequence to the hierarchy of the
Church and to the sacraments themselves? It would appear that
there is no place in the New Theologian's thinking for the Latin
Christian notion of *ex opere operato*, i.e., that as vested with
hierarchical authority by virtue of his ordination, the sacramental actions of a priest will be effective regardless of the condition—virtuous or not virtuous, good or bad—of his soul.
Symeon's intense personalism, his insistence both in the *Letter*
and elsewhere throughout his works[154] on the necessity of
sanctity for the celebrant of the Eucharist and for the other
leaders of the Christian people does seem to bring him "perilously close to Donatism."[155] It is only fair to note that, once
more, he is in this regard scarcely alone in the Christian East.

---

153 See Turner, *Fatherhood*, 57: "...an Eastern Christian spiritual father
    normally views his relationship with the penitent in therapeutic
    terms...[and is] ideally more concerned to help his child attain, perhaps
    after many years, a new and authentic personal relationship with God,
    the result of which will be an inner assurance of divine forgive-
    ness....Finally, it must be noted that...the [contemporary Orthodox]
    formula is deprecatory and not the Western 'I absolve thee.'" However,
    see his qualification in note 75. The deprecatory form does not obtain
    in the Russian Church where, since at least the seventeenth century,
    Western influence has been significant. Thus the two formulae, tradi-
    tional and Western, can be found almost side by side in a contemporary
    Manual of Eastern Orthodox Prayers (Crestwood, 1983), see 55 for the
    traditional form and 59-60 for the Russian usage. For Western influ-
    ences in Russian Christian thought, see esp. G. Florovsky, *Ways of
    Russian Theology* I and II (Belmont, 1979 and 1987).

154 Again, see *H* 58 in its entirety.

155 Ware, "Forward," xxii. He is echoed by Van Rossum, "Priesthood,"
    224, and Maloney, *Fire and Light*, 35.

As early as second and third century Alexandria very similar attitudes are expressed by Clement and Origen.[156] No less a source than Dionysius the Areopagite, inventor around 500 C.E. of the term "hierarchy" and defender of an apparently diametrically opposed (to Symeon) understanding of the relative authority of priest and monk regarding the authority to discipline sinners, says in the same *Epistle* VIII which most directly deals with that question that a priest who is unillumined (*aphotistos*) is "no priest, not at all, but an enemy, a trickster, one fools himself and [is] a wolf amidst the people of God"[157]—a passage which more than one scholar has seen as a prelude to Symeon's own views.[158]

However, while we may speak fairly about a certain danger in the New Theologian's thought, it would be mistaken to read him as a Donatist, a Messalian, or even a tenth-century anticipation of the Protestant Reformation.[159] He may appear occasionally to be "almost" any one of these three, but, to recall Mark Twain's distinction between the lightning and the lightning bug, there is a very great difference between "almost" and "actual." Symeon never extends the logic of his thinking on confession to the other sacraments, and we should recall that confession itself did not enjoy any official status as a sacrament until centuries after his time. Thus again, the alarm sounded by some of his (particularly Roman Catholic) critics is both exaggerated and anachronistic.[160]

156 See Holl, 225-239, for references.

157 *Epistle* VIII.2 (*PG* 3.1092C; Heil and Ritter, 181; Luibheid, 275).

158 St Symeon's relationship to the writings of Dionysius the Areopagite is a topic meriting more investigation than it has usually received. There is some mention of it in Völker, *Praxis und Theoria,* 53, and McGuckin, *Chapters,* 20, and, at greater length, in B. FraigneauJulien's *Les sens spirituels et la vision de Dieu selon Syméon le nouveau théologien* (Paris, 1985), esp. 171-181. See our discussion pp. 168-174 below.

159 So Holl, 102-105, and Darrouzès, *SC* 122, 37.

160 I have in mind particularly Hausherr, *Vie,* (lxxi), Darrouzès, *SC* 122, 28-33; and the whole tenor of Miguel's article, "La conscience de la grâce," summed up in its conclusion, 340-42.

If his opinion on confession and personal sanctity—a very widespread and traditional opinion—never enjoyed official approval by the Church, it is also true that, outside the Western Church, the doctrine of the sacraments as valid *ex opere operato* was not sanctioned teaching either. Indeed, while widely held in the Orthodox Church today, this doctrine still lacks the ecumenical authority accorded the great dogmas affirmed by the Councils of the first millenium. We bring to bear yet another qualification, that it would be quite wrong to suppose that Symeon's failure to apply his logic to, say, the Eucharist or Baptism was mere accident. Throughout his time, and beyond, Byzantium was continually at war with heretical movements of a dualist nature, e.g., Paulicians and Bogomils, which flatly denied the clerical and sacramental apparatus of the Church. The New Theologian was certainly aware of these challenges.[161] All the more significant, therefore, is his assertion, however grudging, in the text quoted above that the ordained have the right to celebrate the sacraments (*hierourgein*), or, in the same text, his explicit statement telling of Symeon the Pious' order that he be ordained. Elsewhere we find him expressing the deepest reverence for the service of the priest before the altar,[162] and his warnings against taking lightly the shepherding of God's people, together with his Eucharistic piety, echo throughout the *Discourses* which follow in these volumes. There is no reason to doubt his sincerity. For him sacraments and priesthood are a divine gift, and therefore to be cherished with the most serious attention to their demand for corresponding holiness on the part of whomever stands before the Holy Table or presumes to approach it. He is certainly not making such statements in an effort to avoid a heresy trial but, as with everything in his works, out of the depths of his own experience.

161 See Turner, "Dualist Heresies."

162 See esp. *Hymns* 14 and 19 on the glories of the priesthood.

It is a difficult thing, even impossible, to be completely balanced and consistent. Some fathers, such as a St Maximus the Confessor, may come close, but they are very rare. The late Archbishop Basil Krivocheine called Symeon "pugnacious,"[163] for example, and the saint refers to himself as a "crazy zealot."[164] Neither, as many have noted, was he a wholly consistent thinker in the tradition of academic theology since the Middle Ages. Some, such as the noted Roman Catholic scholars, Irenée Hausherr and Jean Darrouzès, have deplored this lacuna in his makeup.[165] Their reaction is understandable, and its ancestry goes back a very long way, indeed, back down the centuries through Stephen of Nicomedia to the priest, Amaziah, who confronted Amos before the altar at Bethel.[166] We do not mean to mock a Hausherr or a Darrouzès, but it would not be entirely unfair to see them in their turn as influenced by the debates arising out of the reform and counter-reform, and thus as reading Symeon through spectacles fashioned largely by the sixteenth century. While understandable, this is not really fair either to Symeon or to the tradition of Eastern Christianity which took a different road in resolving—or better, failing to resolve—the age-old polarities existing in the "Israel of God" between mystic and magister, individual and institution, heart and altar, prophet and priest. The Temple at Jerusalem was holy, the place of God's presence and glory which fill it in II Kings 8:11. There Isaiah saw God,[167] and there Ezekiel saw the glory both depart and return.[168] Yet this did not prevent Jeremiah from mocking those who trusted in it,[169] or the same Ezekiel from listing in scathing terms the horrors that

163 Krivocheine, *Light*, 393.
164 See note 4, page 17 above.
165 See note 3, page 30 above.
166 Amos 7:1017.
167 Isaiah 6:15.
168 Ezekiel 10:1-22; 11:22-25, and 43:16.
169 Zechariah 7:115.

defiled it.[170] St Symeon clearly belongs to the line of the prophets
and, like the prophets of ancient Israel, his message occasionally,
even often, leans more heavily toward the "left" side of the
polarities sketched above and earlier than his readers, then and
now, might like or find comfortable. But then, that is precisely the
point of a prophet. Consistency is not the object, let alone philo-
sophical/theological sophistication. The ancient prophets sought
to shock Israel into repentance before the demands of the Covenant. Symeon seeks to confront, as forcibly as he knows how, the
Christian of his time with the demands, and promises, of the New
Covenant:

> For the contemplation of Your countenance is joy;
> For You are not just all good, my God,
> but You as well provide those who look on You with
>   every good thing...
> not only in the world to come—to hell with those who
>   say that!
> but now, even [while] in the body...
> ...You grant that they see you plainly...[171]

From a position of loyalty to the New Covenant community, without departing from the sacraments or denying the
importance of the Church's offices, just as the Old Testament
prophets were loyal after all to Temple and priesthood as
divinely-instituted, St Symeon insists on the reality and imme-
diacy of the Gospel. Christ is risen and the Spirit is poured out
on all who would receive Him. Not to receive Him is culpable
and to deny the possibility of doing so is blasphemy and
heresy.[172] Fine distinctions are put aside. That the lines of
authority are not resolved in this message is quite true, but it is
not Symeon's purpose or his vocation to solve them. The wise
reader will not tarry long in taxing him with this. The tensions

170 Ezekiel 8:5-18.
171 *H* 5.14-21 (M, 279).
172 See esp. *C* 29 on the "heresy of pusillanimity."

his writings underline are in any case insoluble, at least this side of the eschaton. Much better, then, that he should be listened to and taken to heart in order that both heart and mind may be led to worship.

The Shape of St Symeon's Thought

In what follows we shall attempt to present a sketch of the themes which dominate the New Theologian's works, together with occasional references to his sources in the tradition and those modern studies which have examined both this thought and his sources in greater detail. One reason why we feel it unnecessary to refer often to the fathers prior to Symeon, and this is something which is recognized by all his modern commentators, is that he is himself so thoroughly traditional. Shaped by the monastic milieu, steeped in the Scripture, theology, liturgy, and ascetic writings of the Eastern Church, he is at every point the faithful witness, by virtue not least of his own experience, to a continuum of thought and practice which long antedates him. It is, however, also important to state from the outset that any attempt to portray Symeon as a systematic writer is inevitably to distort him. The themes which follow have been extracted from his writings. Never does he himself, as we just noted above, deal with an idea or set of ideas in the organized fashion of an academic. Furthermore, all subsidiary or supporting notes in the melody of his thought are regularly subsumed by, or at least made to dance to, the overwhelmingly dominant theme suffusing virtually his every conscious effort, the experience of God. Everything tends to be telescoped, to collapse into this one, great truth of his life. It breaks into every other consideration, even the most mundane and ordinary, whether a catalogue of ascetic virtues, a list of sins, a talk to his monks on the value of repentance. Yet, it is in that free appeal to his own experience as illustrating and confirming the Church's faith and tradition that he makes his unique contribution, and so it is there that we shall be concentrating much of our attention in what follows, beginning with his understanding of:

The Ascetic Life: Renunciation, the Struggle for the Virtues, and Dispassion.

Renunciation[1] and the Spiritual Father

In his VIth Catechetical Discourse Symeon poses a question which sums up his special combination of the traditional and the personal:

> Unless we become dead to the world and the things in the world, how shall we live 'the life that is hid in Christ' when we have not died for the sake of God? How, as holy Symeon said, shall we contemplate God dwelling in us as light? In no way...[2]

Dying to the world, sharing in the cross of Christ in order to share in His resurrection, is of course a theme which goes back to St Paul and the Gospels. For the New Theologian, this death to worldly ways means first of all the putting aside of one's own will. This in turn suggests to him that the greatest danger facing the Christian, more deadly than the lusts of the flesh and hunger for wealth, is the desire for power:

> You rulers and you rich! Join instead those who are ruled and the poor, since it is difficult for a rich man to enter the Kingdom of Heaven. And, if it is difficult for a rich man, how shall a ruler enter there? Not at all!...Whom does Scripture call a ruler? Someone who seeks his own honor, it says, who seeks to fulfill his own will by ruling...[3]

---

1   For the theme of renunciation (*apotage*) in Symeon and in his sources, see Völker, *Praxis*, 97-111.

2   *C* 6.295-298 (deC, 138).

3   *ED* III.599-609. This is a rather remarkable statement for someone who lived in a society that saw its emperor as the "image of Christ." See Eusebius, "Oration in Praise of Constantine" (*PG* 20.1315C-1440C), and for comment, G.B. Lander, *The Idea of Reform* (New York: 1959),

The Christian is to put aside desire for power and instead seek to do Christ's will, for "who could ever be saved among those who believe in Him who does not do His will?"[4] But how and in what circumstances does one obey Christ and die to the world? For Symeon these questions are answered, in good part at least, by the monastery, though he does add for the edification of his monks the important qualification:

> If instead of being timid, slothful, and despisers of God's commandments, we were zealous, watchful, and sober, we should have no need of renunciation or tonsure or the flight from the world...[5]

While the monastery fulfills the requirement for flight from the world, the tasks of learning Christ's will and accomplishing it remain. If, to some degree, "the monastery environment can serve as guide"[6] to this knowledge, for Symeon the preferred and vastly more effective way is to learn it from another, from the spiritual father:

> Those who have laid down a good foundation of faith and hope, with fear and trembling, on the rock of obedience to their spiritual fathers, and who build without thoughts upon this foundation of submission, and who receive what is commanded them by their fathers as if it had come from the mouth of God, immediately succeed in denying themselves. For, not to fulfill one's own will, but that of one's spiritual father for the sake of God's commandments and of exercise in virtue, ac-

117-132, and F. Dvornik, *Early Christian and Byzantine Political Philosophy* (Washington, D.C.: 1966), 611ff. It also underlies Symeon's frequent warnings against anyone seeking high office in the Church. Here he stands in a long line of monastic writers, e.g., John Cassian, *Institutes* XI.18.

4   *ED* III.599-609.

5   *C* 5.155-159 (deC, 94).

6   K.T. Ware, "The Spiritual Father in Orthodox Christianity," *Cross Currents* XXIV (1974): 310.

complishes not only the denial of oneself, but as well
complete mortification with respect to the world.[7]

The obedience expected is total. Nothing whatever is to be done
without the blessing of one's elder.[8] The latter becomes thus
for his disciple the very presence of Christ:

> When a man has gained a vivid faith in his father under
> God, whenever he looks at him he thinks he is looking
> at Christ Himself...that he is with Christ and following
> Him.[9]

The spiritual father may be the abbot, as Symeon presupposes
in *Catechesis* 20,[10] or a simple monk, as in the case of Symeon
the Pious, but in either case he is "father" to his disciple, "the
one who guides his brother onto the path of spiritual perfection."[11] In *Hymn* 18, Symeon compares the work of his own
elder to that of Moses:

> How shall I tell you, brother, what I have seen in Egypt,
> the marvels and the wonders that he accomplished...?
> The fact is that he came down and found me a slave
>   and a stranger,
> and he said, "Come my child, I will lead you to God."[12]

The office of spiritual father is perhaps most concisely
summed up in the *Letter on Confession* which features a list of
functions that Symeon has taken largely from "The Pastor" by
St John of Sinai:

> Seek out one who is...an intercessor, physician, and a
> good counselor. A good counselor that he may propose
> ways of repentance which agree with good advice, a
> physician that he may prescribe to you medicine which
> is appropriate for each of your wounds; and finally an

7   *ED* IV.151-159.
8   See esp. *H* 4.25ff (M, 22), and *Ch* I.21-30 *SC* 51, 45-48 (McG, 38-40).
9   *Ch* I.28, *SC* 51, 47-48 (McG, 40).
10 *C* 20, (deC, 231ff), and also 18 (deC, 209ff).
11 Christophorides, *Pneumatike Patrotes*, 18.
12 *H* 18.136ff (M, 83).

intercessor that he may propitiate God by standing before Him face to face and offering Him prayer and intercession on your behalf...[13]

In all of this the New Theologian is witness at once to the tradition and to his own life experience. He takes from St John Climacus in the preceding quotation, just as the latter in turn took from a tradition extending back to the Desert Fathers and the New Testament itself.[14] He also, as in the citations above, refers to his experience of the Elder Symeon. It was the latter who led him to God. It was through his elder's prayers that he received his first experience of the divine light,[15] and it was finally his elder whom he saw standing in the midst of that light.[16] Later on Symeon the Pious would confirm a later experience of his disciple, assuring him that this was indeed of God,[17] and our Symeon remained always convinced that it was by his elder's prayers that he had been vouchsafed this grace.[18] The model for the physician, counselor and intercessor, the "friend of God" sketched above, is therefore not merely a literary reminiscence, but a portrait drawn from life.

Yet such persons do not happen along very often. No one knows better than Symeon that for every genuine guide there are a great many more who engage in false advertising. The same passage that describes the true father in God in the *Letter* goes on to warn against the fakes:

Do not go and try to find some flatterer or slave to his belly and make him your counselor and ally, lest, ac-

---

13 *Letter on Confession* 7 (Holl, 116-117). For parallels from John of Sinai's *The Pastor*, see Ware, "Preface," *Spiritual Direction*, xiff.

14 See Völker, 17-29; Turner, *Spiritual Fatherhood*, 39-44; and Christophorides, 15-21. From the *Sayings of the Fathers*, see esp. Poemen 65 and 101, and Synclitiki 17 (*PG* 65.337B, 345D, and 428A; Ward, *Desert Christian*, 176, 181, and 234).

15 See our discussion above, and *H* 37.33ff (M, 197-198).

16 *C* 22.102-104 (deC, 246).

17 *ED* V.287-316.

18 *ED* IX.227-274.

commodating himself to your will and not to what God
wants, he teach you what you want to hear and leave
you in fact an unreconciled enemy. Nor should you
choose an inexperienced physician lest...he plunge you
into the depth of despair or...allow you by inappropriate
sympathy to think you are getting better...and so deliver
you over to...eternal punishment...An intercessor and
friend of God? That, I fear, is not so easily to be
found...[19]

Similar warnings are scattered throughout his work, not a few
of them in the discourses printed below.[20] He likewise provides
his readers on several occasions with a set of criteria for
determining who might serve in this fundamentally "sacramental office," i.e., as an icon of Christ capable of communicating
the Lord to a disciple.[21] Chiefly, the man should give evidence
of a life "in accord with the sacred writings," with the Scripture
and the fathers.[22] Finally he urges prayer. Nothing is more
precious than such a guide. God must be asked for this gift:

Brother, constantly call on God, that He may show you
a man who is able to direct you well, one whom you
ought to obey as though he were God Himself...do what
he tells you and be saved.[23]

Once an elder is found, the way is open. It begins with:

Ascesis

The Nature of the Struggle

Symeon inherits from his predecessors in the monastic
tradition a long-established and enormous volume of writings
on the spiritual life. Characteristic of this literature is first of all

19 *Letter on Confession* 7 (Holl, 117-118).
20 See esp. Symeon's description of the spiritual physician in *ED*
VI.279ff, and I.12.135ff.
21 Turner, *Fatherhood*, 83 and 91.
22 *Ch* I.49, *SC* 51, 53 (McG, 45-46).
23 *C* 20.45-52 (deC, 232).

a profound sense of sin and the roots of sin. As one modern scholar writes concerning the fathers of monasticism: "in the face of God's holiness the conception soon dies out that sin is a matter of individual, avoidable deeds which may be atoned for within a greater or shorter period...Beneath the deeds there lies the ground from which they ascend—tempting thoughts. These above all, these *logismoi*...are the targets of the monastic's struggle. To succumb to them ever again is guilt, always to remain exposed to them is ineluctable."[24] Symeon is fully alive to the necessity of this kind of exacting analysis, as in the following lines from *Catechesis* 25:

>...it is necessary not only to know the turns and changes and alterations that come upon us, but also to know their origins and the manner in which they come—their causes, what winds of thought are blowing, and whence the floods of passions and trials come to assault us. By knowledge of the symptoms we may securely strengthen the house of the soul...[25]

Freedom to conduct this inquiry is one singularly important reason for seeking a life in obedience to a spiritual father or abbot. Such knowledge, Symeon tells us, "comes from a life lived continuously in strict discipline and with a rule."[26] Putting aside one's own will in obedience opens up the possibility of engaging in the warfare to which all Christians are called, "to wrestle first with the demons, our enemies, who are always at war with us."[27]

The ascetic struggle, the ordeal (*agon*), engages the whole person, body and soul, together will all of one's faculties: sensation (*aisthesis*), appetite (*epithymia*), spirited emotion (*thymos*), and reason (*to logistikon*). Drawing on a tradition

---

24 Dörries, "The Place of Confession," 286.

25 *C* 25.200-206 (deC, 272); see also *C* 3.247ff (deC, 66).

26 Ibid. 209-210.

27 *C* 3.314-315 (deC, 68).

which goes back to Plato in the Phaedrus,[28] and at least to
Evagrius Ponticus among Christian monks,[29] Symeon sees the
partial goal of the struggle in the balanced and harmonious
operation of the three powers comprising the soul, such that

>...the reasonable faculty can distinguish the worse from
>the better and indicate to the appetite which things it ought
>relatively to attach itself to, which it should love, and
>which it must turn away from and hate. The emotive
>faculty is situated between these two like a kind of prudent
>servant...raising up resolution to manliness in action...[30]

To arrive at this state, which is nothing less than restoration to the
original and God-intended condition of human existence, requires
a willingness to do violence to the conditions and expectations of
life in a world which has, after all, fallen under the alien rule of
the devil. Thus Symeon, echoing his predecessors, compares the
efforts required of body and soul to flint striking iron:

>Let God take into His spiritual hands your body as a
> stone
>And your soul as a piece of iron
>And let Him draw and push them to do the deeds with
> violence.[31]

For, he adds elsewhere, quoting Matthew 11:12:

>...it was never without many trials and labors, sweat and
>violence, difficulty and tribulation, that anyone was able to
>break through the darkness of the soul or see the light of the
>all-Holy Spirit. "The kingdom of Heaven suffers violence
>and the violent take it by force," since it is through many
>tribulations that we must enter the Kingdom...[32]

---

28 *Phaedrus* 253c-4e.
29 For Evagrius and the use of the tripartite model of the soul, see his
    Kephalaia Gnostica, ed. by A. Guillaumont (*PO* XXVIII, 35; 28.IV,
    73; n. VI, 83 and 85.
30 *ED* IV.404-410.
31 *H* 30.549-555 (M, 171).
32 *C* 6.105-111 (deC, 122).

The Tools of Ascesis and the Virtues

In *Hymn* 30 he spells out the "deeds" of violence:

> What are the deeds...?
>> Vigil and fasting,
>> ardent repentance,
>> outpouring of tears and contrition [*penthos*],
>> the continual remembrance of death,
>> unceasing prayer
>> and the patient bearing of all sorts
>> of trials that come one's way.
>> Above all, silence
>> and profound humility...[33]

Although this list comprises a kind of rough hierarchy,[34] it remains the case that all these activities of body and soul are necessary, part of the working out of salvation which all are called to accomplish. Fasting is the foundation of all life in the Spirit, as Symeon tells us in *Catechesis* 12, the ground of sobriety (*nepsis*).[35] It roots the monk in self-control (*engkrateia*) and endurance, the training of the will in the virtues which he calls elsewhere the monk's voluntary imitation of the martyrs.[36] Avoidance of sleep in prayer (vigil—*agrypnia*), the total of four or five hours of rest a day that he prescribes in *Catechesis* 26,[37] is another traditional element of monastic life, more training of the body in obedience to the soul. The same holds for the constant recollection of death,[38] "sleeping on the ground and a hard bed, non-possession and abstinence from

---

33 *H* 30.556-565 (M, 171).

34 Unlike other writers, such as Climacus or Evagrius (though he is doubtless dependent on them), Symeon does not offer anywhere in his writings a precise ordering or "ladder" of passions or virtues. However, see *Ch* I.13, *SC* 51, 43 (McG, 36).

35 *C* 12.81ff (deC, 175ff).

36 *ED* X.566ff.

37 Sleep is divided between a midday nap of perhaps two hours (*C* 26.246ff), and another three hours or so at night (Ibid. 292ff).

38 See, for example, *C* 21.

bathing, and everything which follows from these."[39] Again in *Catechesis* 26, we find him outlining a complete day for his monks, one marked by hours in church, limited food, a minimum of conversation, and constant attention to the motions of the heart—a rigorous, even harsh discipline.

Yet these virtues or tools are only the beginning of the effort, the most outward and least important—if still indispensable—rungs of the "ladder." While they are necessary, they are never to be taken as themselves sufficient. They are "like dead bones fastened to one another,"[40] are "nothing at all, because many indeed among the evil-doers and the wretched have endured such things...neither ceasing from their evil nor improving their wickedness."[41] The body is to be disciplined and its passions—gluttony, lust, avarice[42]—to be placed under controls, but the deadlier temptations of pride and anger, listlessness, despondency, and vainglory (to complete the traditional eight[43]) require stronger and more piercing medicine. The heart, understood as the center and depth of the human being, must also be touched and transformed in order for the filth of sin to be burned away, the wound it has caused cleansed, and the devil who lodges within the wound expelled.[44] Here, in the softening and washing clean of the heart, is the realm of another set of virtues. Here, too, although God's presence and aid is never lacking at any point in the process,

39 *ED* VII.321-324.

40 Ibid. 324ff.

41 *ED* VIII, ll.175-8.

42 Evagrius ranks these three, gluttony, lust, and avarice, as physical passions, i.e., as pertaining to appetite (*epithymia*), see the *Praktikos and Chapters on Prayer* (Kalamazoo: 1981), pp. 16-17. See also Symeon on avarice in *C* 9.92ff (deC, 152-153), for one of the strongest denunciations of "property" in patristic literature.

43 Evagrius. The "eight evil thoughts" became traditional in the ascetic literature of the East. See J. Špidlik, *The Spirituality of the Christian East* (Kalamazoo: 1986), 248-254.

44 See *ED* IX.325ff.

we enter more perceptibly into the sphere of co-operation with Him and, in so doing, into the possibility—which Symeon sees as always the goal of every human striving—of our perceiving Him. This is the level of ascesis which the New Theologian refers to most often as, simply, "doing the commandments," and for him it comprises the forecourt of the King:

> ...he who is continent in every respect and has trained his soul not to wander in a disorderly manner, nor to follow its own will...but instead ardently compels it to traverse all of God's ordinances, this man will shortly find Him Who is hidden within His divine commandments. And, when he meets Him, forgetting every other activity...he will have no other desire than to look upon Him...[45]

To stand before the face of God's holiness is first and last an act of faith. Faith is therefore the beginning of every ascetic effort and of all the virtues. It is the ground and context of beatitude:

> ...it is faith...which mediates between both, I mean between God and man, so that, although we are poor and possess nothing whatever by which we may enter into our salvation, God has mercy and accepts our faith in Him in place of everything else, and so freely grants us forgiveness of our sins, deliverance from death and corruption, and freedom. The latter, indeed, He bestows...on all who believe in Him with all their soul, and not just that, but as well everything else which He has promised...that He will make us new again and renew us by water and the Spirit, will number us with His servants, the saints...and will Himself be united and joined with us...[46]

This passage might almost have been written by one of the Reformers, by a Luther or a Calvin. Symeon, however, is neither.[47] Human freedom, the role of the will in accepting or

45 *ED* VI.102-109.

46 *ED* XIII.166-181.

47 Thus Holl, 92.

refusing salvation, is axiomatic for him. He recoils, as is evident in *Ethical Discourse* II, from the notion of predestination. His insistence on the necessity of human effort is equally constant. Faith and works are both indispensable, but it is the first which operates the latter:

> ...just as tools without the workman and the workman without tools are unable to do anything, just so neither is faith without the commandments, nor the fulfillment of the commandments without faith able to renew and re-create us.[48]

Faith initiates the effort, stimulates the fear of punishment and hope of reward,[49] and, as it grows and effort increases, reveals our human dependence on divine mercy:

> You know, O Master, I never trusted in my works or
>   deeds for my salvation.
> But it was only in Your mercy, O Lover of Mankind,
>   that I sought refuge,
> having confidence that You would save me freely...[50]

This revelation of powerlessness, of human weakness and dependence, together with the sweetness of God's mercy, is the real point of the ascetic way. Self-knowledge, the guarding of the thoughts and denial of appetite, work through faith to reveal the depths of our alienation from God, of our sin, and our utter inability to approach Him without His first coming down to us. To reflect in faith on the abyss of God's mercy revealed in the incarnation, death and resurrection of Christ, as does Symeon in the opening lines of *Discourse* VIII, is to be led to love for Him.[51] Here is the root of his anger in *Discourse* II at those who would hide from ascetic labors by arguing for predestination. They are avoiding work, refusing faith, and

48 *ED* I.12.159-63.

49 See *Ch* I.13, *SC* 51, 43 (McG, 36).

50 *H* 42.48-51 (M, 217); see also 26.93-96 (M, 141).

51 *ED* VIII.1-57.

excusing their sins. "Where," he asks, "did you learn you did not belong to those who are foreknown and predestined?...Who told you this?" and he continues: "Why do you rather not believe that, having been slaughtered for your sake, He will never abandon you...?"[52] Here, too, is the wellspring of repentance (*metanoia*), of contrition (*katanyxis*) and compunction (*penthos*), of tears and humility. These terms, all related and implying one another, are so frequent in the New Theologian's works that it would be pointless to list them. All of them are embedded in the spiritual literature from which he draws[53] and, typically, belong as well to the fabric of his own experience. Again and again he calls his monks to repentance in his *Catechetical Discourses*.[54] Repentance is nothing less than renewal of the baptismal grace all have fallen away from since infancy.[55] It is accompanied—rather, signaled by—a piercing of the heart in which grief for sins is combined with the fire of longing. This is compunction, compounded of water and fire:

> ...like water because it quenches all the fire of passion with tears and washes the soul clean of stains, and [it is] like fire which gives life by the presence of the Holy Spirit. It kindles, blazes up, and warms the heart and inflames it with love and desire for God.[56]

Water and fire at once belong to the order of created being and are types of the uncreated. Love (*eros*) and desire (*pothos*) are both human faculties, emotions or drives to which Symeon refers frequently in his works.[57] Human, too, are tears and

---

52 *ED* II.1.153-166.

53 See esp. I. Hausherr, *Penthos: the Doctrine of Compunction in the Christian East*, trans. by A. Hufstader (Kalamazoo: 1982).

54 No less than five of the *Catechetical Discourses*, numbers 4, 5, 11, 23, and 30, are dedicated to the theme of repentance.

55 See, for example, *H* 15.251-261 (M, 57).

56 *Ch* III.12 *SC* 51, 83 (McG, 75). See also *H* 28.129-131 (M, 150).

57 See, for example, *C* 1.91ff (deC, 43ff); *H* 39.1ff (M, 202); 42.74ff (M, 218); 16.23-33 (M, 58); *Ch* III.30-32, *SC* 51, 89 (McG, 75); and *ED* IV, *SC* 129, 70.

grief. But mingled with these virtues, the higher rungs on the ladders of ascesis, there is always the presence of Another. To ask for compunction, for example, is in Symeon's view the same as calling for God's indwelling:

> Give me compunction, your life-giving drink,
>
> The drink that penetrates the perceptions of my flesh and soul,
>
> The drink which makes me joyful always and gives me life.[58]

Just as "it is impossible for the body to do anything without the soul," he writes, "so is the soul unable to be moved and to keep the commandments without the Spirit."[59] The virtues are always a compound, a blend of human and divine. Only sin is completely our own.[60] At times Symeon will speak of the virtues and the human faculties of soul and intellect as combustible matter awaiting the kindling of the Spirit,[61] while at others he will declare the virtues simply names for the Spirit Himself at work in us, since "He does not possess His own name among men."[62] The thought is in any case consistent, insistent, and paradoxical: without grace there are no virtues, and without our doing of the commandments there is no grace.[63] Though infinitely unequal, God and man are still partners, co-workers. The perception of this infinite inequality is itself another key virtue for Symeon. This is humility, another fruit of repentance. Humility and faith are cast as the "feet" of the body of virtues described in *Ethical Discourse* IV, the foundation of all the virtues that follow: non-possession, obedience, prayer, endurance, compassion, bearing of

58 *H* 26.103-105 (M, 141).

59 *H* 47.25-28 (M, 239).

60 See, for example, *H* 24.127-128 (M, 129). Not even sin is wholly our own since it requires assent to evil and the evil one. Symeon knows no neutral place.

61 See *H* 30.78-87 (M, 161), and 33.130-139 (M, 186).

62 *H* 22.176-179 (M, 111).

63 See *Ch* III.52, *SC* 51, 95 (McG, 87).

burdens, patience in affliction, the consolation of others—the last four of which comprise the suffering for, and imitation of, Christ.[64] Throughout, humility is a constant theme, the virtue whose growth ripens into a fruit which is not of this world.[65]

Symeon has several names for the complete complement of the virtues. It is the "body of the mature man in Christ," purity of heart, the "wall" against the passions, the "bodyguards" of the soul, the "vessel" or receptacle of the Holy Spirit.[66] Each of the last three serves to illustrate his insistence that the observance of the commandments must be complete. If there is a hole in the "vessel" grace leaks away; if a crack in the wall, or a missing guard, thieves and murderers break in and destroy. He never tires of repeating that it is possible to keep all the commandments since, by denying this, one would be calling the Lord a liar.[67] Yet, typically, he is fully aware that human weakness is in constant need of divine strength, as in the following passage on the struggle against the passion of listlessness (*akedia*):

> ...If God allowed it to work its full power against us, no ascetic would ever be saved. So while we should resist it according to our ability, it is for God to awaken us mystically and clearly give us the victory over it...[68]

More is implied in this quotation than God's silent and unnoticed assistance. The "organic link between ascetic and mystical themes is a regular feature of Symeon's teaching."[69] The battle with the passions is governed by his desire for the "union

64 See also *C* 6.301ff (deC, 127).

65 See esp. *H* 17.99-115 and 236ff (M, 62 and 65ff).

66 For "body of the mature man," *ED* IV.369ff; for purity of heart, *Ch* III.29 and 35, *SC* 51, 88-90 (McG, 80-82); for "wall" against passions, *ED* IX.453-475; for "bodyguards" of soul, *Letter on Confession* 4 (Holl, 112-113); for "vessel" of Holy Spirit, *C* 27.67-98 (deC, 286).

67 For example, see *ED* X.219ff.

68 *Ch* I.74, *SC* 51, 60 (McG, 53).

69 Krivocheine, *Light*, 39.

with Christ to become ever more intimate," such that the struggle is always linked in his mind with its necessary culmination in the vision of the glory of the Risen Christ.[70] Thus the body of virtues is merely a handsome corpse[71] unless arrayed with the "life-bearing mortification of Christ,"[72] and a pure heart is nothing more than an empty chamber "unless the love God [has] been poured richly in it"[73] and Christ appears therein "reflected like the light of a lamp in a mirror...a light which is personal and substantial...seen invisibly and comprehended incomprehensibly."[74] The Christian is called to the freedom of the children of God, the original glory lost in Adam, and the perfect reflection of God's love. Thus we arrive at the summit of the virtues, the entry within the King's palace:

Dispassion (*apatheia*) and Love

Dispassion is not an originally Christian term. It comes from Stoic philosophy and, like the related terms "untroubledness" (*ataraxia*) and self-sufficiency (*autarkeia*), signified an inner freedom from the passing cares and upsets of life, a kind of indifference to weal and woe which derived from one's acceptance of his or her place in the world.[75] When Christian writers, beginning with Clement of Alexandria in the late second century, took up the term its meaning began to shift toward signifying liberation from the dominance of the fallen world.[76] For the monastic tradition, it is in particular with Evagrius of Pontus (d. 399) that the word truly comes into its

---

70 Völker, *Praxis*, 230.

71 *H* 50.162-71 (M, 253-254).

72 *ED* IV137-138.

73 Ibid. 645-646; see also V.106-164.

74 *ED* X.885-889.

75 See Špidlik, Spirituality, 267-281, and G. Bardy's article on *apatheia* in *Dictionnaire de Spiritualité* 1.727-746. For an illustration of the idea, if not the term itself, in late pagan thought, see Plotinus' portrait of the philosopher, unmoved by the cries and alarms of this world, in *Enneads* III.2.15 (Loeb ed., 90-94, lines 22-62).

76 See Stromateis VI.9.71-72, (GCS 2 Bd. Stromata, Buch I-VI, 467).

own and becomes a fixed star in the constellation of Christian virtues. Unlike the Stoics, however, it is never considered in isolation, but instead is always linked with love. Dispassion and love are seen as "two aspects of a single reality...the one supports and vitalizes the other, enabling its continuance and full expression. They are, as it were, the positive and negative poles of a single field of force."[77] Within this "force-field" the human faculties of appetite, emotion, and reason are stabilized and allowed to function as they were originally intended to do. Human nature is restored and rendered capable of reflecting the uncreated love which brought it into existence and which, in Christ, has redeemed it. From the first appearance of Christian monasticism and, particularly in the Christian East, ever since the fourth century, the person reckoned dispassionate (*apathes*) is venerated as *pneumatophore*, as a witness to and vehicle of the Holy Spirit.[78] St Symeon is no exception.[79]

While the linkage of dispassion to love as a single force is primarily Evagrius' contribution to the spiritual tradition, another line of development, less intellectualist than the first, made little mention of the first element. Concentrating rather on the second, love, and on its locus in the human heart, this second line is represented at first chiefly by the fifth-century collection of writings known as the *Macarian Homilies.*[80] While these are not without controversy, especially in modern times,[81] it is unquestionably the case that they were received

---

77 E. Bamberger, *The Praktikos*, lxxxv and, more generally, lxxxii-lxxxvii. For Evagrius, see Ibid. 14.

78 See, for example, S. Brock, "Early Syrian Asceticism," 13ff, and, relatedly, P. Rousseau, "Spiritual Authority," 382-387.

79 Thus Gouillard, *Quatre Procès*, 11, for the stress on *apatheia* in Symeon's day.

80 Text from H. Dörries et.al., *Die 50 Geistlichen Homilien des Makarios* (Berlin: 1964). Trans. by G. Maloney, *Pseudo-Macarius: The Fifty Spiritual Homilies and the Great Letter* (New York: 1992).

81 For "Macarius" as Messalian, see H. Dörries, *Die Theologie des Makarios-Symeon*, (Göttingen: 1978) and A. Louth, *The Origins of*

by the Eastern Church as legitimate expressions of the Christian faith. For "Macarius," the heart is the true center of the human being.[82] Christ descends into the human heart to do battle with the devil and his angels.[83] The heart is again the place where love, the presence of Christ, wells up within and transfigures the human person, and it is finally there that one encounters Christ as light.[84] These themes are taken up by another fifth-century writer, Mark the Ascetic,[85] the very writer whom Symeon is asked to read by his elder at the beginning of their acquaintance.[86] The two currents, Evagrian and Macarian, meet and merge to a degree in such later writers as Isaac of Syria[87] and John Climacus.[88] Maximus the Confes-

Christian Mysticism: From Plato to Denys (Oxford: 1981). In defense, see J. Meyendorff, "Messalianism or Anti-Messalianism? A Fresh Look at the 'Macarian Problem,'" *Festschrift für Johannes Quasten* II, (Münster: 1970), 585-590. Note also Krivocheine's balanced remarks in *Light*, 31, note 19. We look forward as well to the publication of the paper on the Messalian question delivered at the latest conference (May, 1992) of the North American Patristics Society by P.M. Blowers. The latter's view is essentially the one sketched in a few words by Archbishop Basil, i.e., that the Messalian "heresy" was represented by ascetics generally orthodox in intent, but who suffered in being tarred with the brush of minority elements who went beyond the pale of accepted behavior and preaching. See also the latest publication on Messalianism and the Macarian Homilies, C. Stewart's *Working the Earth of the Heart* (Oxford: 1992), esp. 67-69, for the conclusion that much of the issue of "Messalianism" stems from a Greek mis-reading of idioms common to Syriac-speaking Christianity.

82   E.g., *Hom* XV.20-21 (Dörries, 139-140; Maloney, 116).

83   *Hom* XI, 11 (Dörries, 103-104; Maloney, 95).

84   *Hom* VIII.3-4 (Dörries, 78-80; Maloney, 81-82).

85   See the article by K.T. Ware, "The Sacrament of Baptism and the Ascetic Life in the Teaching of Mark the Monk," *SP* 10 (1970): 441-452; and, for Mark himself, *Against Righteousness by Works*, in the *Philokalia* I, 98-138, esp. 113 and 115 (Greek. ed.). For the English trans., see *Philokalia* (Ware, Sherrard, and Palmer) I, 131-132.

86   *Vie* 4, (6).

87   See M. Hansbury's remarks in *St Isaac of Nineveh: The Ascetic Life* (Crestwood: 1989), 16-18.

88   See the *Ladder*, Steps VI.13; VII.2; XV.55 (esp.) and XV.64, Greek

sor (d. 662), while keeping a basically Evagrian orientation with the latter's preference for the intellect (*nous*) as the locus of the encounter with God, also corrects Evagrius by placing particular stress on love as "the blessed passion" and the very indwelling of God Himself.[89]

These lines of tradition come fully together in Symeon's own thought. In *Ethical Discourse* IV he provides us with an example and summary of his predecessors' works in a singularly striking image. He is trying to describe the interplay of dispassion and love in the Christian saint:

> So then, picture with me the sky as it is on a clear and cloudless night. See, there is the moon's disk, full of limpid and purest light, and around it the halo which often appears. Now, with this in mind, turn your thoughts to what I am about to say. Each one of the saints, while yet in the body, is like that evening sky and the heart of each like the moon's disk. Holy love is the all-efficacious and all-powerful light, far and incomparably greater than the light of our sun, which touches their hearts and, working in accordance with the capacity of each, fills them perfectly. Neither does it ever wane, like the light of the moon, but is always kept all light through the zeal and good works of the saints. And holy dispassion, like an aureole and a tabernacle, surrounds and cares for them, covers them completely, and preserves them unwounded by every evil thought—let alone by sins—and sets them up as unhurt and free from all their foes...[90]

The same discourse provides us with Symeon's most complete

(Athens: 1970).

89 See I.100; II.6; III.1000 and IV.100 in his *Centuries on Love*, *PG* XC.981D-4A, XC.985BC; XC.1048A, and XC.1073A; English in P. Sherwood, *St Maximus the Confessor on the Ascetic Life and the Four Centuries on Charity*, *ACW* 21. Note also the latter's remarks in his "Introduction," 91-99.

90 *ED* IV.769-786.

statement of this summit of the virtues. The passage just cited
is a distillate of that discussion and of the New Theologian's
understanding of the Christian life as our realization of the
potential, lost in Adam and restored in Christ, for life with and
in God. It is worth a look in more detail.

Symeon begins the *Discourse* by insisting that freedom from
evil, specifically from "evil lust" and "impassioned thoughts" is
necessary even to think of dispassion. One must have a clear eye
to see the light. He goes on to speak of progress in the virtues,
sketching a kind of ladder of perfection with reference to both
dispassion and to the virtue which he understands as linked—and
to a degree synonymous—with it, humility.[91] Thus, and here he
is quite unusual, he admits to degrees of dispassion:

> Dispassion of the soul is one thing and dispassion of the
> body another...One thing is immobility of the body's
> members and even the soul's passions, quite another the
> possession of the virtues. While the former derives from
> nature, the latter has the habit of suppressing all the
> natural motions...[92]

These degrees are paralleled immediately by those of humility:

> It is one thing to speak humbly, another to think hum-
> bly, and humility is one thing while the blossom of
> humility is another, and yet another the latter's fruit and
> the beauty of that fruit, and still another the energies
> which come out from it...[93]

These two virtues represent, in short, human existence as a
union of our effort and God's grace. Both elements are constant
and necessary:

> Of these, some are proper to us, and some are not. It is

---

91   The two are closely allied in one of Symeon's chief sources, *The
     Ladder*, Steps XXV and XXIX.

92   *ED* IV.65-71. See also *Ch* I.86-90; *SC* 51, 66-67 (McG, 58-59).

93   Ibid. 85-88, and see also *Ch* I.91-92 and III.7-25; *SC* 51, 67-68 and
     82-88 (McG, 59-60 and 74-79).

our part to conceive, think, reason, say and do everything which brings us toward humility. Holy humility...and the rest of its characteristics, its charismata together with its energies, are God's own gift. They do not belong to that which is ours...No one, however, will ever chance to be made worthy of these gifts unless first, like laying down seeds for them, he does everything which is his to do.[94]

Grace is won when it is sought for with all one's strength, with constant repentance and prayer. It is never earned, but is always a gift which is entirely incommensurate—the gift being infinite—with the paltry work of human efforts. Symeon thus compares God to a gracious emperor who gives generously when His servant shows gratitude.[95] And the gift is extraordinary. He "gives them His entire self" as raiment, as the "robe of glory," and as food and drink.[96] This, Symeon continues, is the true wealth of the Father Who trains His sons by temporarily depriving them of His presence in order to bring them to repentance, to sorrow, and to longing for Him.[97] The struggle against the passions and for the virtues is nothing other than our education in how and what to desire, a focusing of human energies and passions on their intended goal, the treasures of the Father beside which everything earthly is scrap and carrion.[98]

The middle of the discourse lays out Symeon's picture, touched on above, of the complete or "mature man" in Christ, the body of the virtues.[99] In an extended metaphor, he likens the different limbs and organs of the human body to the virtues of the perfected Christian. Faith and humility, as we have seen,

94 Ibid. 89-96.
95 Ibid. 22-24.
96 Ibid. 254-279.
97 Ibid. 280-312.
98 Ibid. 314-330.
99 Ibid. 370ff; and cf *Eph.* 4:13.

correspond to the feet. Ankles, calves, knees and thighs answer
to non-possession, nakedness, voluntary exiled, obedience and
service. The sexual organs are represented as "unceasing
prayer of mind,"[100] the sweetness of tears and joy of the heart
in consolation—a kind of transfiguration of *eros* to which he
will return at the conclusion of the discourse. Kidneys and hips
signify constancy in prayer while the digestive system corresponds to the capacities of the intellect, here identified explicitly with the heart. Nerves, sinews, muscles and fat have their
analogues in meekness, simplicity, forbearance, and compassion. He pauses at this point for a digression on the human
composite, especially the three faculties of the soul, as an
image of the Holy Trinity, and we shall take this up again
below. The metaphor then continues by comparing chest, back,
shoulders, arms, hands and neck—he deliberately leaves out
certain organs and their corresponding virtues for "those who
choose to seek out knowledge of them by experience"—to,
respectively, alms-giving, bearing the burdens of others, patience and endurance, the readiness and zeal for the commandments, and unwavering hope.

The body of the virtues corresponds to the moon and sky in
the image we began with above and, like the moon without the
sun, it is dead and inert without its "head." While these virtues,
Symeon tells us, are themselves the fruit of "co-operation with
the Holy Spirit," they are still lifeless, stale, unable to cohere
and live without that life which is beyond them. It is the head

100 Ibid. 375-378. Symeon's use of *nous* (intellect) here—the whole phrase
in fact—recalls Evagrius' definition of prayer as "the communion of
the mind with God" (*On Prayer* 3). He does, though, link it clearly with
the heart. While he does not spell out the nature of the "unceasing
prayer" that he refers to here (unlike the fourteenth-century hesychasts
who link it with the "Jesus prayer") it is not impossible that he could
have had the latter in mind. The practice of repeating the name of Jesus
was not unknown to his predecessors. Thus see I. Hausherr, *The Name
of Jesus*, trans. by C. Cummings (Kalamazoo: 1978), 265-308.

which quickens the whole and makes it capable of drawing breath, receiving nourishment and attaining to growth. The head is "holy love" and, he continues, "this love, the head of all the virtues, is Christ and God."[101] Love for Symeon, as one modern critic writes, is therefore "not merely an attribute of God, but the substantial presence of God."[102] The New Theologian is never merely a moralist. Love signifies a sharing in Christ's "divinity by which we are made one with God."[103] In the first of his *Catechetical Discourses*, he echoes Revelation 20 in calling love "the one city, the kingdom of heaven...its glory is inaccessible, its counsels unsearchable...beyond time...this holy Zion not made with hands."[104] Here, in short, is the glory of the world to come. To be sure, it is veiled as Christ's divinity was veiled by His humility and His crucifixion. Thus the saints willingly endure the mortification of their own flesh in imitation of Christ. Yet, they are at the same time "wholly with God" Who "abides consciously in them and they...consciously in God."[105] These are the only ones who merit the title "dispassionate." They are preserved from evil and confirmed in grace and the assurance of the Father's treasures. They "live their lives on earth as if they were in heaven."[106]

At this point, following an ironic comparison of people who play at the possession of dispassion with little boys who play at soldiering, Symeon introduces his image of the full moon as "a type of what is actually being perfected in us."[107] It is in full accord with our summary of the tradition of dispassion and love

101 Ibid. 548-550.
102 Stathpoulos, *Die Gottesliebe bei Symeon, dem neuen Theologen* (Bonn: 1964), 35.
103 *ED* IV.555-557.
104 *C* 1.53-9 (deC, 42).
105 *ED* IV.658-661.
106 Ibid. 687-688.
107 Ibid. 761-768.

as the twin poles of a single reality. That reality is "the sun of righteousness shining within us...the new earth and new heaven."[108] Here, in this heaven revealed within the heart, is the true object of the heart's longing, the place where eros finds its intended fulfillment—the "private parts" of the body of the virtues. The saints, Symeon writes, "will never have enough, never be satisfied with the contemplation of that beauty...always increasing in sweetness and kindling their desire."[109] This is also, then, the realm of the spiritual senses,[110] where perception is no longer enslaved to the power of sin but finds itself harnessed to the activity of God within and made new.

Finally, for Symeon the dispassionate are not called simply to a private pleasure. They are meant to be "Spirit-bearers" to their fellows, "real and effective teachers for our less attentive brethren."[111] He is insistent on this point in *Discourse* IV and particularly so in *Discourse* VI, since in the latter it is his own elder and the latter's state of grace that he is defending. Symeon the Pious was truly *apathes*, and as such a true teacher and spiritual physician.[112] Thus we find here as well the core of the New Theologian's battle with the authorities of his time. Against them he insisted that this state of existence, this beatitude and freedom, is fully open to attainment in this life, and

108 Ibid. 826-828.
109 Ibid. 866-869.
110 See Fraigneau-Julien, *Les sens spirituels*, 142ff.
111 *ED* IV.832-834.
112 Symeon the Pious is nowhere mentioned by name in *ED* VI, but the whole discourse is devoted to the defense of the proposition that someone can "arrive at such a height of humility that he may dine with a woman without yielding to some injury or suffering in secret some impulse or stain," and that such a person will further not be injured by "circulating in the middle of towns...and seeing people laughing and dancing," nor be affected even were "his naked body" to be "in contact with [other] naked bodies." These characteristics—converse with women, circulation in the city, lack of shame at nakedness—match those we noted above as marking the elder Symeon's vocation as "holy fool."

therefore that the *pneumatophoroi* of old—a Paul, an Antony, a Macarius—have their equivalents in the present day. It is not an accident, then, that he concludes *Discourse* IV with an appeal to his own experience of God: "This is the blessed passion that we, too, a cast-off, have by God's grace...been deemed worthy of suffering."[113] Typically, he offers his own experience as the touchstone and proof of the ascetic and spiritual tradition. That experience was at once in accord with prior writings on ascesis and the virtues, and, as Symeon repeats untiringly, a living and lived reality:

> We have received by experience, in perception, in vision and in knowledge, everything in which we have discussed, and have set this down in writing for the edification and encouragement of all who seek God and long to find Him. Share this our suffering, therefore and pray with us...[114]

What is it that he claims he has experienced? He replies: "the simple light of divinity."[115]

---

113 *ED* IV.925-928.
114 Ibid. 929-933.
115 Ibid. 862-863.

The Vision of God:
St Symeon the Mystic

The struggle of the ascetic and the very economy of God's salvation find their meaning for Symeon in the "harvest of grace," deification. This is the heart of his message to his monks, the core of his experience and calling as a prophet, the content of the Christian Gospel: that God may be known and lived now, and that in knowing Him we may see and share the glory of the Trinity. We shall touch on the importance of the term "glory" below, its place in the tradition upon which Symeon draws, and later move to a consideration of the role the sacraments and Church play in his understanding of *theosis*. We begin, however, with his experience itself.

The Glory

Reports of the Experience

It is not possible to pin down precisely the number of times St Symeon was visited by the apparition of the divine light.[1] His writings and Nicetas' *Life* suggest that this grace was not infrequent, if varied in its intensity. Nicetas, for example, claims that, on the occasion of his master's ordination to the priesthood, the latter saw:

> ...the Holy Spirit as an infinite and formless light descending upon him [and he continued]...throughout the forty-eight years of his priesthood to see Him descend on the sacrifice he was offering to God whenever he celebrated the Liturgy...[2]

1   See esp. Julien-Fraigneau, *Les sens spirituels*, 144-145.

2   *Vie* 30, (40).

There are, however, at least two, and perhaps more, occasions of which we do have a clear and unambiguous witness. First there is the experience Symeon had while still a youth, the story of "George" which he tells us in the third person in *Catechesis* 22 and which Nicetas repeats in the *Life*.[3] On this occasion the young man was overwhelmed, "lost all awareness of his surroundings and forgot that he was in a house... He saw nothing but light all around."[4] As we saw above, he subsequently not only fell away from the light, but gave up the cultivation of prayer altogether for some years. His next reported encounter appears to have been during his brief stay at the Studion Monastery while under the immediate and intensive care of his elder. He reports this experience, again in the third person, at least twice: once in *Catechesis* 16 and in *Discourse*.[5] In the latter account, he notes a combination of wonder and ignorance. The young man "sees light." While on the one hand he is amazed at what he has seen, on the other he does not know immediately who it is who has been revealed to him. The novice (Symeon) then runs to his spiritual father, who had "told him beforehand about such things, as having known God from before." The elder asks, "What did you see, child?" and the disciple replies, "Light, O my father, sweet, sweet!" So sweet, indeed, that the young man declares, "I was moved to streams of tears." The elder then confirms the other's experience. "It is He, child," and the novice, following the old man's confirmation, is led to further revelations:

> ...he sees Him again and, little by little, comes to be completely purified and, purified, grows bold and asks that One Himself, and says, "My God, is it You?" And He answers and says, "Yes I am He Who for your sake

3   Ibid. 5, (8).

4   *C* 22.92-93 (deC, 246).

5   *C* 16.78-144 (deC, 200-202); *ED* V.287-316; see also *C* 35.113-195 (deC, 362-365), and 36.147-254 (deC, 372-375).

became man. And behold, I have made you, as you see, and shall make you God."[6]

This second account, particularly the passage just quoted, almost certainly represents a "telescoping" or compression of visions experienced over a considerable period, perhaps even years. Notable is the role of Symeon the Pious at the earlier stages, the process of purification, and finally the growth from wonder and amazement before the Presence to conversation and dialogue between Creator and creature, and the prospect of future growth to come: "I shall make you." This is an altogether admirable sketch in narrative form of the Orthodox doctrine of deification. It rests upon the economy of Christ ("for your sake became man"), involves a process of learning (the elder), ascesis ("comes to be purified"), and finally permits a boldness before God (the dialogue) and growth in fellowship with Him which, accomplished once and for all in Christ, appears to have no limit or end. Yet it is also the account of a lived experience, not a theory but a report.[7] Symeon's vocabulary throughout all his writings underlines this insistence. It is an "experience" (*peira*), a term with a history in patristic literature,[8] and one which the New Theologian usually reinforces with terms such as "perceptible" (*aisthetos*), "conscious" (*gnostos*), in "contemplation" (*theoria*) and "knowledge" (*gnosis*).[9] He insists at the same time on its transcendence. It is "supernatural" (*hyperphyos*), an event which is neither controlled by its subject nor in any way predictable, but which instead is "suffered" (*pathein*).[10] It is always "sudden" (*aiphnes*),[11] unexpected and in complete command. In one

6   *ED* V.311-316.
7   See Julien-Fraigneau, 152-159, and P. Miguel, "La conscience de la grâce," 314-320.
8   See Lampe, *A Patristic Greek Lexicon* (Oxford, 1961), 1055; and P. Miguel, "*Peira*" 355-361.
9   See Julien-Fraigneau, and Krivocheine, *SC* 96, 151-154.
10 Miguel, "La conscience de la grâce," 319-320.
11 Extremely frequent in Symeon's writings, for example "George's" vision

extraordinary passage from his *Theological and Ethical Chapters*, he compares it to a flash of lightning:

> Suppose a man were to stand inside a house at night with all the doors shut. he opens a window and, suddenly, a flash of lightning wraps him round with its brilliance. His eyes cannot bear the flash...it is the same with the soul enclosed by the senses. If it leans outside, as if through the window of the mind, it is dazzled by the lightning flash of the pledge within it (I am speaking of the Holy Spirit) and it cannot bear the radiance of this unbearable light...[12]

We do have examples of Symeon using the first person, as in the passage we quoted at the end of the previous section, in speaking of his experiences. These instances, however, lack the specific times and settings we are given in the accounts of "George" or the "novice" above. Still, it is possible to note certain details. The visitations usually take place while he is at vigil, praying alone in his cell during the night. Besides the night vision of "George," Symeon tells of God appearing to him while he is sitting and reading in his cell,[13] standing before the icon of the Theotokos,[14] praying

in *C* 22.90. It is, of course, perfectly likely that Symeon is simply reporting here, but one can find an ancestry for this term in connection with the moment of sudden insight—or the experience of God—going back a very long time in the history of Greek literature. See the article on the related term, *exaiphnes*, by W. Beierwaltes, "*Exaiphnes* oder die Paradoxie des Augenblicks," *Philosophisches Jahrbuch* LXXIV (1966-7): 271-283, where the writer argues that Plato's use of the term in the *Parmenides* (and elsewhere) was taken up by Dionysius Areopagita in the latter's *Ep* 3 (*PG* 3.1069B), and adapted to the Christian mystery of the Incarnation. (See also A. Golitzen, *Et Introibo ad Altare Dei: The Mystagogy of Dionysius Areopagita* [Thessalonica: 1994], 223-227.) If, as we feel is the case and as we argue below, Symeon had read Dionysius and valued him, this is perhaps a case of terminological influence. Yet another instance, in other words, of the New Theologian's combination of the personal and the traditional.

12   *Ch* III.54; *SC* 51, 96 (McG, 87-88).

13   *H* 13.63-68 (M, 45-46), and 25.42-67 (M, 136).

14   *C* 36.265-272 (deC, 376).

the Trisagion,[15] or, as in Nicetas' account, while celebrating the Eucharist, which would appear to have some support in the *Discourses* printed below.[16]

The Experience

Growth

Symeon sees the Christian life as growth into God's light. The language of ecstasy, wonder and bewilderment, of being dazzled, is very common in his writings. Elsewhere he will speak of being seized with vertigo (*illigio*),[17] but it is also clear that ecstasy and stupefaction are not the end of the story. There are degrees to this experience. On some occasions it is over-whelmingly powerful while at others it seems to tantalize. In *Hymns* 22 and 51 in particular, Symeon speaks of the light waxing and waning, appearing first as a star, then growing until it is like the sun in brilliance, and finally once again withdraw-ing.[18] Secondly, there is no end to its possible depths. In a striking phrase from *Hymn* 1, he calls the divine light an "abyss of progress,"[19] and goes on to declare that it leads to a perfec-tion which is ever incomplete, i.e., perpetually open to and demanding further completion, increase without end.[20] Thus, thirdly, the experience of God is not limited to rapture. To the

15 *C* 16.78-86 (deC, 200).

16 See particularly his insistence on the necessity of consciously perceiv-ing the grace present in the Eucharist in *ED* III.525-554, X.754-774, XIV.248-280, as well as in *H* 14.55-74 (M, 48-49).

17 For example, *H* 11.71 (M, 37).

18 *H* 22.5-18 (M, 107), 51.1-29 (M, 258), and see also *C* 16.129-134 (deC, 202).

19 *H* 1.180 (M, 15).

20 Ibid. 180-214 (M, 15-16); see Krivocheine, *Light,* 386, and also, for the notion of a perpetual longing for God, ED IV.866-869. In the latter, Symeon denies the possibility of ever being satiated with God (*koresthenai*), an idea he certainly owes to Gregory of Nyssa's doctrine of eternal ascent into God (*epektasis*). For the latter, see P. Deseille, "Epektase," *Dictionnarie de Spiritualité* 4.785-788, and J. Daniélou, *From Glory to Glory*, trans. by Musurillo, (Crestwood: 1979), 56-71.

contrary, ecstasy belongs to its initial stages. It is the reaction
of a beginner and not of a master in the spiritual life. This is the
burden of the argument he presents at greatest length in the
twelfth chapter of *Discourse* I below, and which he illustrates
with the allegory of the prison. A man who has been impris-
oned all his life in impenetrable darkness suddenly glimpses
the light of the sun through a chink in the prison wall. He is at
first completely dazzled by what is totally unfamiliar. Gradu-
ally, however, his astonishment begins to recede as he becomes
used to the light, his natural element, and he starts to pick out
details and learn of the great world outside the confines of his
cell. It is the same, Symeon argues, in the case of the soul.
"Rapture of the mind does not apply to the perfect," he says,
"but to beginners." When the initial stage is over and the soul
continues to live in the light, it is then "initiated into and taught
wonders upon wonders, and mysteries upon mysteries."
Knowledge increases-of oneself, of others, and of God. Such a
person, he notes elsewhere, no longer even needs the books of
Scripture and writings of the fathers, but "himself becomes a
divinely inspired book for others...the same One Who inspired
the scriptural writers abides within this man as his intimate."[21]
Rapture is the beginning of a relationship with the infinite God
which can and should expand forever.[22]

Light

For St Symeon the encounter with God is expressed primarily in terms of vision. The verbs of seeing-*blepein*, *oran*,
theasthai-and related nouns predominate.[23] The saint sees
God, and what he sees is the light "proper to the divine nature

21   *Ch* III.100; *SC* 51, 112-113 (McG, 102-103).

22   For a parallel in the life of a nineteenth-century saint, see the conversation
      between Seraphim of Sarvo and Nicholas Motovilov in G. Fedotov's *A
      Treasury of Russian Spirituality* (Belmont, Massacussetts: 1975), 266-279.
      Though in the light of God, both Seraphim and his interlocutor converse
      quietly and calmly.

23   Julian-Fraigneau, 152.

(*ta tes theias physeos idia*)."[24] In *Discourse* V below he is arguing his familiar case against people who talk about God without having seen Him. It is, he says, like someone going on at length about the sights of a city he has never visited. Only the person who has been there can speak authoritatively. He continues:

> It is just the same with regard to the Jerusalem on high and the invisible God Who dwells within it, or concerning the unapproachable glory of his countenance, or about the energy and power of His all-Holy Spirit, in other words, His light. No one can say anything unless he has first seen the light with the eyes of his soul and knows precisely its illuminations and activities as they occur within himself...

Hearing about God is simply not enough, for

> ...how could merely hearing bring about the knowledge of God in us? God is light, and the vision of Him is as light ...whenever someone sees Him revealed, he sees light.[25]

There is nothing impersonal about this encounter, either. The light, as Symeon is fond of repeating, is personal (*phos enhypostaton*), or, more specifically, light in three Persons (*phos trishyposta-ton*).[26] It is the grace and revelation of "the glory of the Lord Jesus Christ through the gift of the Holy Spirit."[27] He returns often, as again in the twelfth chapter of *Discourse* I below, to the promises Christ makes to His disciples in John 17:22:

> [Christ] Himself points out this very truth most clearly when He says: "The glory which You have given Me I have given to them..." Don't you see that the glory given by God the Father to the Son before the ages [a reference to John 17:5] is given by the Son Himself to the saints, so that they may all be one?[28]

24 *TD* III.134ff (McG, 138).
25 *ED* V.263-276; see also 251-258.
26 For example, *ED* I.12.300-302.
27 *ED* X.481-486.
28 *ED* I.12.294-296.

The whole thrust of his argument in *Discourse* III below is that St Paul, whom he takes as the great paradigm of the mystical experience[29] and whose experience reported in II Corinthians 12:2-4 he is commenting on, saw God as light, "the light beyond light ...supremely unknowable glory and divinity of the Son."[30] In this single word, light, Symeon understands "all the manifestations of God, all His charismatic gifts, and the charismatic life itself."[31]

The last statement deserves elaboration. The following list is not exhaustive, but it will give some idea of the range of associations the light of God has for the New Theologian. It is light which invests the saint, crowns his virtues with dispassion,[32] and fulfills his desires beyond hope or expectation.[33] It is the very desire itself for God, the personal presence of the Holy Spirit.[34] It chases away the passions, banishes the powers of darkness,[35] and consumes the marks and stains of sin.[36] At the least trace of sin it withdraws and leaves longing and grief behind, until patience and repentance call it back again.[37] It opens up the depths of the scriptures and makes the saint himself "scripture."[38] It gives him boldness (*parresia*) before God, the boon of speaking to Him as friend to friend and of interceding on behalf of others.[39] It is the tree of life and the flowers of Paradise.[40] It is the robe and crown of glory which

---

29   *ED* III.396ff; see also *H* 11.75-77 (M, 38), and Völker, *Praxis*, 400.
30   Ibid. 125ff.
31   Krivocheine, *Light*, 237.
32   See *ED* IV.662ff, and VI.216ff.
33   Ibid. 254-267, and see also *Ch* III.21; *SC* 51, 86 (Mc, 77-78).
34   *H* 52.3-6 (M, 263).
35   *H* 33.38-42 (M, 184).
36   *H* 51.1-17 (M, 258); see also *ED* X.778ff, and VII.551ff.
37   Ibid.
38   *ED* VII.427ff; X.361ff; *Ch* III.100; *SC* 51, 112-113 (McG, 102-103); and *C* 24 on the "treasure chest of spiritual knowledge" in its entirety.
39   See *Letter on Confession* 14 (Holl, 124).
40   *H* 47.3-20 (M, 239).

Adam lost in Eden, and which Christ recovered on Calvary and offers us again in Baptism.[41] It is a shimmering pool of water[42] and the "ineffable sea of glory," the infinite ocean, into which we are called to descend.[43] It is the presence now of the world to come,[44] the foretaste and pledge of the eschaton,[45] here in our midst as it shall be on the last day.[46] The light is God, before and embracing all creation,[47] and the tiny mustard seed which is planted and hidden in the heart of each.[48] It is the single ray of divinity which contains the universe[49] and the intimate communion of God Alone with the soul alone.[50] While known most intimately in the depths of the heart, it remains a mystery, unknowable and ineffable.[51]

In *Hymn* 22, God tells Symeon not to seek out either His nature or the energies of His Holy Spirit, their "how" or "why."[52] The light itself is sufficient. It is both that which is seen and the instrumentality by which the created soul is given to see, just as "visible light is at once the object seen and the medium of sight itself."[53] The initiative therefore always belongs to God, never to Symeon. By the light, in the midst of it wondering, he sees the light: "by grace I received grace."[54] The

41 *ED* XIII.198-205, and *H* 55.28-74 (M, 279-280) in the context of repentance as the renewal of Baptism; see also *ED* III.310-374.
42 *CD* 36.147-54 (deC, 372).
43 See *Ch* II.11-19; *SC* 51, 74-77 (McG, 65-68), and relatedly, *H* 23.283ff (M, 119-121).
44 *ED* X.706-725.
45 *Ch* III.50; *SC* 51, 94-95 (McG, 86).
46 See *C* 18.293-298 (deC, 217).
47 *H* 53.71-89 (M, 268).
48 *H* 17.773ff (M, 76), and 28.93ff (M, 149).
49 See *H* 25.52-60 (M, 192).
50 *H* 27.71-79 (M, 142; AK, 70-78).
51 *H* 50.13-30 (M, 250).
52 *H* 22.148-165 (M, 110).
53 *H* 2.98-105 (M, 19); see also *ED* XIII.262-273, and *C* 2.353-364 (deC, 56). In the latter text, one contemplates God's glory in that glory.
54 *C* 17.33-36 (deC, 205).

light transforms and makes all that it touches into light. In *Hymn* 16, Symeon speaks of his face and of all his members becoming "bearers of the light (*photophora*),"[55] and in the preceding hymn he spells this out in terms which astound and shock the reader even today—to the degree, indeed, that this hymn was not included in the edition put out in the 1780's by Nicodemus the Hagiorite and Dionysius Zagoraios.[56] Yet his logic is clear and unassailable. In *Hymn* 17 he thanks God because, after fervent repentance, "You purify and illumine [us], and make [us] participants and communicants in Your light and divinity."[57] This participation in the light of divinity is not limited to the soul or intellect. The body shares in it as well.

The Whole Man Deified: Nuptial and Other Images of the Union with God

The deification of the whole man is a necessary consequence for Symeon of the Incarnation of the Son of God. The New Theologian appears to be completely free of the old Platonist fear and distrust of the body which had afflicted such earlier Greek Christian writers as Origen and Gregory of Nyssa,[58] or for that matter, of Augustine of Hippo whose strictures on the body's capacity for God continued to influence Western Christianity on the subject of the beatific vision throughout the Middle Ages and beyond.[59] Symeon accepts instead the fact that God Himself "was not ashamed" to become like one of us and, in consequence, has shared Himself with us in every particular, and in every member of the body. To shudder at all the implications of the last, as he says to

55 *H* 16.33 (M, 58).

56 See Koder, *SC* 156, 19-20.

57 *H* 17.66-68 (M, 61).

58 For Origen, see the study by J. Daniélou, *Origen*, trans. by Mitchell (New York: 1955), esp. 216-219; and for Gregory, idem, *Platonisme et théologie mystique* (Paris: 1944), 48-59. For Gregory's doubts about sexual reproduction, see *de hom. opf.*, *PG* 44.188A-192A.

59 See Lanne, "L'Interprétation palamite," esp. 42-43.

his opponents in *Hymn* 15, is to

> ...attach your shame to Christ and to me
> saying: 'Do you not blush at these shameful words,
> and above all to bring Christ down to the level of
>   shameful members?' [i.e., the sexual organs]

Symeon replies at once:

> But I say in my turn: "See Christ in the womb of His mother,
> picture to yourself the interior of this womb and
> He escaping from it, and whence my God had to pass to
>   come out of it!"

and thus concludes:

> ...He accepted all that for our glory...
> He became totally man, He truly and completely God
> ...and the same One is completely God in the
> totality of His members...[60]

He is, of course, aware that this boldness was startling, not to say disturbing, to his contemporaries, and that it was easily subject to misinterpretation. One might recall at this point the unusual aspects of Symeon the Pious' sanctity. Both Symeon's insistence on the whole man deified and the defense of his elder come together in his argument in *Discourse* VI. In arguing for the effects of dispassion and its real presence in the saints, Symeon insists that the latter truly are transfigured and, as he continues in *Hymn* 15, united to Christ. It is Christ Who restores their integrity, such that what was

> ...formerly soiled by corruption, in their eyes
> is no longer, but [is] sanctity, incorruption, perfectly healed.
> ...They are entirely united to His total love;
> or rather, by receiving as we have already said, His holy
>   seed within themselves, they completely possess God
> Who has taken the form of man.[61]

---

60 *H* 15.192-204 (M, 55-56).

61 Ibid. 225-231 (M, 56).

The light of Christ permeates the whole man. Thus liberated from the sway of passion and sin, the saint is free to reflect God perfectly in every aspect of his being.

These three themes—the divine light, dispassion, and the imagery of sexual union—come together in a remarkable passage in *Hymn* 46:

> ...dispassion in the form of lightning united itself with me
> and ever more remains—understand this spiritually,
> you who read, lest you be wretchedly defiled!—
> and produces in me the ineffable sweetness of consummation
> and an infinite longing for marriage, for union with God,
> sharing in which I, even I, have become dispassionate,
> who was enflamed with passion, afire with longing for it,
> and I partook of the light, yea and became light,
> beyond every passion and outside every evil.[62]

Archbishop Basil Krivocheine rightly notes that "the theme of mystic marriage with its nuptial imagery is not unknown in Greek patristic texts," and he singles out in particular SS Gregory of Nyssa, Dionysius the Areopagite, and John Climacus. Still, he continues, St Symeon is different "because of the audacity and daring realism of his descriptions," borrowed as they are from "physical love and the physiology of the human body."[63] Yet the saint's boldness is always grounded on the bedrock of the Incarnation, whose completeness he insists, must be reflected in the transformation of "the entire human body."[64]

---

62 *H* 46.29-37 (M, 237). For the combination of dispassion and the erotic, see also *H* 9.24ff (M, 33-34).

63 Krivocheine, *Light*, 369.

64 Ibid. 370.

Elsewhere, and particularly in the discourses printed below, nuptial imagery and faith in the Incarnation are extended to include the picture of a kind of doublet, the repetition, of Christ's nativity occurring in the believer. In chapters nine and ten of *Discourse* I, Symeon argues that the "sacred marriage (*hieros gamos*)" of Mary the Virgin with God is repeated in the saints, such that each is to feel the living Word within and carry Him as a pregnant woman feels and carries the child within her womb.[65] The image is not original with St Symeon,[66] but it is developed with his usual force. He is, of course, careful to insist on the uniqueness of the Theotokos, but in a way that is without prejudice to his appeal to all Christians to share in an experience like hers. True, she alone bore God in the flesh, but all are called to the mystical marriage in the Spirit and to receive within themselves the seed which is the Word. Reversing this imagery and comparing the believer elsewhere to child and lover, he speaks of the latter feeding on the breasts of God,[67] though here, too, he is drawing on a tradition extending back into Christian antiquity.[68] Consistent throughout these images is a boldness, a lack of shame or embarrassment with regard to the human body and its share in the economy of Christ, and to its "adequacy" thus for the things of God, that is at once peculiarly Symeon's own and consistent with the tradition out of which he writes.

He also draws on other, perhaps less disturbing images. In the concluding section of *Catechesis* 23, the subject of a valuable study by Archbishop Basil,[69] he takes up the equally

65 See esp. *ED* I.10.179-185; and also both *ED* X.860-865, and XI.167ff.

66 See the *Sayings of the Fathers*, Longinus 5, *PG* 65.257B (Ward, 123).

67 CF *H* 28.183 (M, 151); *ED* X.859, and IV.269-277.

68 At least as far back as the second century; see the *Odes of Solomon* XIX.2-5, trans. by S. Brock, *The Apocryphal Old Testament*, ed. H.F.D. Sparks (Oxford: 1984), 709.

69 "Le thème de l'ivress spirituel dans la mystique de saint Syméon le nouveau théologien," *SP* 5 (1962): 368-376.

long-established imagery of wine and drunkeness for the experience of God, mingling it with his characteristic emphasis on light. Speaking of the joy which comes with God's healing grace after the affliction of ascetic labor in repentance, he compares those trials with a winepress, and the product of human struggle and divine grace with "wine that has been strained and held up against the sun," then continues:

> I do not know which pleases me more, the sight of the sun's rays and the delight of their purity, or the drinking and the taste of the wine that is in my mouth ...so that I am not sated with seeing nor filled from drinking
>
> ...the beauty of the rays that pass through it redoubles my thirst and I crave it again...and I am inflamed by the thirst and desire for that most transparent drink.[70]

This thirst, he adds, "will never be quenched for all eternity."[71] The wine and the light express the union of creature and Creator. In this union the wounds and "putrefaction" of the fallen soul and body are healed, i.e., the notion of dispassion is implicit, and so restored are both the "taste" already of another reality, and of a relationship without limit. The glory of God is available now.

The Glory in the Tradition

Throughout all of his works Symeon insists that this experience of God's glory is the same as is maintained by the Scripture and the fathers:

> ...If we have views different from those of the apostles and of the holy, God-inspired fathers ...if we fail to repeat what the Holy Gospels say about God, then let us be anathema... Instead, however, we restore the teachings of the Master and the apostles that some have perverted.[72]

70 *C* 23.158-170 (deC, 258).

71 Ibid. 173-174.

72 *C* 34.248-263 (deC, 354).

It is time to ask to what extent he is justified in making such a claim, or in asserting, as for example he does in *Hymn* 25, that the glory which he beholds is the Holy Spirit,[73] Whose light, as he says elsewhere, streams from Christ as light from the sun.[74]

Moving first to the witness of Scripture, it is clear that St Symeon has a certain basis for his assertions. The glory of God, the *kabod* in the Hebrew texts, is obviously connected with God's self-manifestation.[75] It is the glory which leads Israel out of Egypt as fire and cloud[76] and which later descends on the peak of Sinai with storm and lightning.[77] It fills Solomon's Temple at the latter's dedication.[78] Isaiah sees it in the Temple,[79] and Ezekiel sees it both leaving the sanctuary on the eve of Jerusalem's fall and returning to it in the days of the city's [idealized] reconstruction.[80] Its place is particularly above the mercy seat of the ark of the covenant and it is dangerous to approach, as the children of Israel are warned in Exodus 19, Aaron in Leviticus 16:2, and as both Aaron's sons and Uzzah find to their cost.[81] In Exodus and Ezekiel particularly, it is given the appearance of a radiant, fiery substance, thus the accounts in Exodus 24:5ff and especially 34:29-35 where Moses descends from his encounter on the mountain with his face veiled to hide the glory's reflected light. By the time of the Septuagint translation into Greek, the term *doxa* has "acquired its distinctive sense as a term for the divine nature either in its invisible or its perceptible form."[82] In later Old

---

73 *H* 25.36-39 (M, 136).
74 *H* 1.141-146 (M, 14).
75 See the articles, *DOXA*, by G. Kittle and G. von Rad in *The Theological Dictionary of the New Testament*, vol. II, 232-255; and "Gloire," by P. Deseille in *Dictionnaire de Spiritualité* 6. 422-463.
76 Ex 13:21-22 (though the word "glory" is not used).
77 Ibid. 19:9 and 16, and 24:16-17.
78 I Kg. 8:10-11.
79 Is. 6:1-5.
80 Ezk. 10:18-22, 11:22-23, and 43:1-5.
81 Lev. 10:1-3 and II Sam. 6:4-7.
82 Kittel, *TDNT* II.244.

Testament books, reflected for example in Daniel 12:3, the blessed in the age to come are believed to share in the divine glory, and this becomes a frequent theme in apocalyptic literature.[83] Philo of Alexandria, a Jewish platonist and contemporary of St Paul, will speak of the divine glory as that which comprises the vision of God for human intelligence, as opposed to the divine essence which is forever hidden.[84]

The same tradition is at work in the New Testament. St Paul is knocked off his horse and blinded by a sudden vision of light.[85] Stephen the protomartyr sees the glory of God and Christ as he dies.[86] In the Apocalypse of John, the glory of God lights the New Jerusalem.[87] St Paul once again refers to Christ as "the Lord of glory"[88] and, in comparing the experience of Moses on Sinai with that of the Christian, states explicitly that the Christian's is the superior and perfected vision of the same glory: "And we all, with unveiled faces, beholding the glory of the Lord, are being changed into His likeness from one degree of glory to another."[89]

All three Synoptic Gospels record the Transfiguration of Christ, and this event comprises perhaps their clearest statement that the Old Testament theophanies find their fulfillment in Jesus. Moses and Elijah appear speaking with him as each did before with God on a mountain top.[90] Here again, although the word itself is absent, the themes associated with the divine

---

83 See, for example, Sebastian Brock's introduction to *Hymns on Paradise,* (Crestwood: 1990), 66-72, on the theme of the "robe of glory" prominent in St Ephrem of Syria's writings. The latter seems to have taken it from late Jewish thought and passed it on in turn to later writers such as Symeon.

84 See *de Spec. leg.* 45-47, *Quest. et Sol. in Exod.* II. 45 and 47.

85 Acts 9:3-4.

86 Ibid. 7:55.

87 Rev. 15:8 and 21:23.

88 I Cor 2:8.

89 II Cor. 3:18.

90 Mk. 9:2-4; Mt. 17:1-3; and Lk. 9:28-32. The last verse of Lk. 9:32, states that the disciples "saw his [Christ's] glory."

glory are evident: the light, the cloud, and their stunning effect on the disciples.

The Gospel of John, which together with St Paul is Symeon's favorite source, makes the association between Christ, the glory of God, and the Christian believer perhaps most explicit of all. That the Word becomes flesh and "tabernacled (*eskenosen*) among us,"[91] spells out what is implied in the synoptic narratives of the Transfiguration, i.e., that Jesus is the "place" of the glory as the Temple was in the Old Dispensation. Moreover, the same glory which Christ says He shared with the Father "before the world was" in chapter 17:5, He says He has given to the disciples in verse 22: "I have given them the glory You gave to Me." It is therefore not difficult to see how Symeon could read these texts as explaining his own experiences, nor how he could then link the latter, and the glory itself, to the coming of the Spirit which Christ promises in John 14-16, to the Spirit's appearance as tongues of fire at Pentecost in Acts 2, and to the fulfillment of God's promises to dwell among His people such as we meet in, for example, Romans 8. The Spirit and fire of God, Christ in light and glory and the indwelling Trinity, are finally summed up for Symeon in the promise Jesus makes to His disciples in John 14:21, a verse which he quotes continually: "anybody who loves Me will be loved by My Father, and I shall love him and show Myself to him."

While we shall return below to the Trinity, here we note once more that Symeon's reading of these texts was far from original. He claims the fathers as his witnesses, and he has a solid case.[92] The Second Epistle of Peter is regarded by most

91 Jn. 1:14.

92 See, for example, the emphasis on the Transfiguration in V. Lossky's study, *The Vision of God*, trans. by A. Morehouse, (London: 1963), esp. 35-37 and 67ff. See also J.A. McGuckin, "The Patristic Exegesis of the Transfiguration," *SP* 18 (1985): 335-341. The most extensive investi-

New Testament scholars as having been written sometime in the early to mid-second century.[93] If we accept this, we find the Transfiguration continuing to be accorded prominence in the Church of that period, together with the assurance that Christians shall become "partakers of the divine nature."[94] In the 180's St Irenaeus of Lyons, who is not especially given to statements on the inner, subjective aspects of the spiritual life (that would come later, with the great Alexandrines), still lets slip a remarkable statement in his *Adversus Haereses*. This remark allows, at the least, for the belief that a certain tradition regarding the Transfiguration existed in the Church of Lyons, a tradition which held that the light which shone from Christ at that time is available to the believer now. The Word was made flesh, says Irenaeus, and conquered death in order that

> ...all things...might behold their King; and that the paternal light might meet with and rest upon the flesh of our Lord, and come to us from His resplendent flesh, and that thus man might attain to immortality, having been invested with the paternal light.[95]

Just after this remark, Irenaeus further recalls the New Theologian, eight centuries later, when he insists that the vision of God as light is both available in the Holy Spirit, and that it is life:

> ...the Spirit [is] truly preparing man in the Son...and the Son [is] leading him to the Father...For as those who see the light are within the light, and partake of its brilliancy, even so, those who see God are in God, and receive of His splendor. But [His] splendor vivifies them; those therefore who see God do receive life.[96]

gation of the latter theme is probably G. Habra's *La Transfiguration chez les pères grecs*, but I have been unable to avail myself of it.

93 The *New Jerome Biblical Commentary* (1990), 1017-1018, places it ca. 100 AD.

94 II Pet. 1:4 and 16-18.

95 *Adv. Haer.* IV.xx.2 (*SC* 100, pt. 2, 630; *ANF* I, 488).

96 Ibid. IV.xx.5 (*SC* 100, pt. 2, 638-640; *ANF* I, 480-489).

Around the turn of the third century Clement of Alexandria will also argue that the knowledge of God, which is His gift of Himself, "comes to us in the manner of light (*kathaper phos*) penetrating the soul entire."[97]

In the literature of the monastic movement this theme of light or glory is present from the time of the very earliest witnesses we possess. The first "theoretician" of the spiritual life, Evagrius of Pontus, writes for example of the peak of the Christian ascetic's experience as "essential knowledge" of the light of the Trinity,[98] and elsewhere warns against investing the divinity with any form or shape[99] precisely as Symeon does six centuries later: the light of God is "altogether without form, wholly simple, uncompounded, undivided in nature."[100] In language less influenced by the vocabulary of late Platonism and redolent instead of the scriptures, the Desert Fathers make the same point. While always cautious about visions and apparitions,[101] the earliest monks affirm the possibility of seeing God in this life.[102] Abba Arsenius in fact links the vision of God with the believer's inner life, and in terms recalling Symeon's own favorite text, John 14:21: "If we seek God, He will manifest Himself to us, and if we keep Him, He will remain close to us."[103] This statement is borne out in a story about Arsenius. One of the other brothers happens by the old

---

97 *Stromateis* VII.7 (*PG* 9.453A), and see esp. the mysterious *Excerpta ex Theodoto* 4-5 (*SC* 23, 58-63) which make explicit reference to Mt. Tabor and the light of divinity.

98 *Kephalaia Gnostica* I.35 (Guillaumont, *PO* XXVIII).

99 *On Prayer* 66 and 70 (Grk. *Philokalia* I: 178 and 183; Eng. *Phil.* I: 58 and 63, also Bamberger, 66).

100 *H* 22.159-160 (M, 110).

101 In the *Sayings of the Fathers*, see for example Antony 2, Arsenius 27, and Zacharias 5 (*PG* 65. 76B, 96BC, and 180C; for English, Ward, 1, 13, and 68).

102 As maintained by P. Rousseau, *Ascetics and Authority*, 28, and "Spiritual Authority," 386.

103 Arsenius 10 (*PG* 65. 89C; Ward, 10).

man's cell and sees him "entirely like a flame."[104] Abba Silvanus is interrupted in his vision of the glory of God, and another time is seen by someone else as reflecting its light.[105] Abba Sisoes dies in its radiance,[106] and the Abba Joseph, on being asked by Abba Lot what the latter had to do to be saved,

> ...stood up and stretched out his hands toward heaven. His fingers became like ten lamps of fire, and he said to him, "If you will, you can become all flame."[107]

Antony himself, the father of monks, was said to have been "borne up by the Spirit (*pneumatophoros*),"[108] and, in the sayings ascribed to him by the *Philokalia* (admittedly of doubtful authenticity), refers to the "fire of the Holy Spirit" which he has received.[109] In the same collection, Mark the Ascetic, whom we may recall Symeon was given to read by his elder, insists on the endowment of the believer of all the gifts of the Holy Spirit,[110] and on the possibility here-below of being filled with the divine light.[111]

The most singular parallels to Symeon's writings in early patristic literature belong to the late fourth-century *Macarian Homilies*, which continued to be widely read in monastic circles.[112] In *Homily* IV, "Macarius" argues that God does

---

104 Arsenius 27 (*PG* 65: 96BC; Ward, 13). Note that the monk who sees the old man "light up" is qualified by the narrator as one who was "worthy of this sight."

105 Silvanus 3 (*PG* 65. 409A; Ward, 223). See also idem, 12 (Ibid. 412C; Ward, 224).

106 Sisoes 14 (Ibid. 396BC; Ward, 214).

107 Joseph of Panephysis 7 (*PG* 65.229CD; Ward, 103).

108 Antony 30 (*PG* 65.85B; Ward, 7).

109 In the collection, *Early Fathers from the Philokalia*, trans. by Kadlubovsky and Palmer, (London: 1954), 78.

110 Ibid. 65.

111 Ibid. 78.

112 See J. Meyendorff, *A Study of Gregory Palamas*, trans. by G. Lawrence, (London: 1964), 136-138; and G. Maloney's Introduction to *Pseudo-Macarius: The Fifty Spiritual Homilies*, 20-22.

make Himself visible, and he uses the example of Moses to make his case.[113] In *Homily* V, Moses is a type of the glory Christians may enjoy through the Holy Spirit,[114] while *Homily* XII insists that the same glory even now may be found within the believer, and it specifically singles out the Transfiguration as its model.[115] The writer speaks elsewhere[116] of the vision of glory in light, of his own experience of the same[117]—a first person anticipation of Symeon—and, although he sets it in the world to come, his meditation on Ezekiel's vision in *Homily* I recalls the dazzled wonder of young "George" in the midst of glory, having become "all light, all eye."[118]

This language continues in subsequent writers. Maximus the Confessor in the seventh century writes of God's eternal blessings that, given dispassion, the believer may "even in the present life begin to taste of these blessings,"[119] and elsewhere that, at the summit of Christian life, divine grace brings "to rest the natural actions of the body... then God alone shines through both body and soul, vanquishing their natural features with overwhelming glory."[120] His contemporaries, John of Sinai, whose *Ladder* became required reading for Eastern monks ever afterward,[121] and Isaac of Syria, whose work was appearing in Greek translation for the first time just before Symeon's birth, reflect the same emphases. John, like Symeon at the end of *Discourse* VII,

113 *Hom.* IV.10 and 13 (Dörries, 34-35, 37; Maloney, 54-56).

114 *Hom.* V.10-11 (Dörries, 61-63; Maloney, 73-74).

115 *Hom.* XII.12 and 14 (Dörries, 113-114; Maloney, 101-102).

116 For example, *Hom.* VIII.1-3 (Dörries, 76-80; Maloney, 81-82).

117 Ibid. 6 (Dörries, 83; Maloney, 83).

118 *Hom.* I.2 (Dörries, 1-2; Maloney, 37-38). Compare Symeon, *Ch* II.11ff, esp. 19 (*SC* 51, 74-77; McG, 65-68).

119 *Centuries on Charity* IV.78 (*PG* 90.1068B; trans. by Ware et al, *Philokalia* II, 110).

120 *Gnostic Centuries* II.88 (*PG* 90.1168AB; Ware, *Phil.* II, 160). Maximus, however, is talking about the eschaton.

121 It is required reading to this day for all Eastern monks during the Great Lent. Symeon became acquainted with it early, see *Vie* 6, (10-12).

describes different states of receptivity to the fire of God:

It is one thing frequently to keep watch over the heart and another to supervise the heart by means of the mind...when the holy and super-celestial fire comes to dwell in the souls of the former... It burns them because they still lack purification, whereas it enlightens the latter according to their degree of perfection. For one and the same fire is called both the fire which consumes and the light which illumines...[122]

And, concerning the person who has attained to dispassion, he writes that this virtue

...so sanctifies the mind and detaches it from material things, that for a considerable part of life in the flesh ...a man is rapt as though in heaven, and is raised to divine vision...[123]

Isaac of Syria is rich with references to such experiences, and it is surely no accident that Symeon so often echoes him.[124] Concerning the knowledge that comes from God, Isaac writes that "it manifests and reveals itself in the innermost depths of the soul itself, immaterially, suddenly, spontaneously, and unexpectedly."[125] Yet, though immaterial and "unseen by physical eyes," he warns that "you must not doubt and think that He is not there, for He often becomes manifest even to physical eyes."[126] The illumined intelligence "clearly sees the

122 *Ladder* XXVIII.51. The latter is according to the numbering in the English version put out by Holy Transfiguration Monastery, (Brookline, Massachusetts: 1978), 218-219. In the Greek version, (Constantinople: 1883, rep. Athens: 1970), it is XXVIII.52, p. 63. Note the expression "unfinished perfection (*atelestos teleiotes*)."

123 Ibid. XXIX.5, 221 (Gr. XXIX.3, 165).

124 Völker, *Praxis*, 94-95, 148-149, 159-161, 168, 197, 211, 214, 220-221, 403, 421, 431-432, and 448.

125 Isaac 49, *Early Fathers from the Philokalia*, 190. For a translation directly from Syriac, and thus a more certain source, see *The Ascetical Homilies of St Isaac the Syrian*, Holy Transfiguration Monastery (Boston: 1984), *Homily* 53, 264.

126 Ibid. 119, *Early Fathers*, 216; *Ascet. Hom* 72, 354, and see also *Hom*

glory of Christ,"[127] and this experience Isaac links, quoting John 14:15-16, further on with the gift of love and reception of the Holy Spirit:

> The coming of the Comforter means the gift of the revelation of spiritual mysteries; therefore in receiving the Spirit ...lies the whole perfection of spiritual knowledge.[128]

Like Symeon later, and in concert with a long line of predecessors, he takes St Paul as the exemplar of the Spirit-bearer:

> It was precisely when the blessed Paul received the Holy Spirit and was renewed by Him that he was granted the mysteries of revelation...heard ineffable words, saw visions transcending nature...as he himself wrote in his Epistle to the Corinthians...[129]

In *Discourse* III below, therefore, Symeon is putting together elements long extant in the tradition. His interpretation of St Paul's experience in II Corinthians 12 contains, in isolation, no one thing which is new. Doubtless, here is the reason why St Gregory Palamas will make good use of it three centuries later.[130] Symeon's particular emphasis on the Apostle's expe-

15, 86, and 43, 213-215. *Homily* 15 appears to have been written in the eighth century by John of Dalyatha, but was-we should think-in the text which Symeon read. For John and his striking anticipation of the main themes in later Byzantine hesychasm see R. Beulay, "Formes de lumière et lumière sans forme. Le thème de la lumière dans la mystique de Jean de Dalyatha," in *Mélanges Antoine Guillamont* (Geneva: 1988), 131-141, and by the same author, *L'enseignement spirituel de Jean de Dalyatha* (Paris: 1990), esp. 440-464.

127 Isaac 146, *Early Fathers*, 226; *Ascet. Hom.*, Appendix B, 437. According to the latter's introduction, xci, this and the following two citations are from the "Epistle to Abba Symeon" written by Philoxenus of Mabboug around 500 AD. Again, however, Symeon is likely to have read them simply as the work of Abba Isaac.

128 Ibid. 148, *Early Fathers*, 227; *Ascet. Hom.*, 440. For a work that is Isaac's own, and around the same theme, see *Asc. Hom.* 37, 182-183, and 53, 203.

129 Ibid. 155, *Early Fathers*, 230; *Asc.Hom.*, 444.

130 See p. 182, note 27.

rience as light is, perhaps, new, but the themes contributing to this interpretation are all well established.

We should like to bring one last witness to this cursory overview of light and glory in the fathers, the singularly important eighth-century figure of St John of Damascus. The latter's *Homily on the Transfiguration*[131] is, if not identical to Symeon's own writings, then so close to him as to indicate another of his sources. In the light of the Father's Spirit, John says, we "see the light unapproachable, the Son of God." What was formerly invisible is made manifest, and "an earthy body flashes with divine brilliance, [from] a mortal body flows [the] glory of divinity."[132] In the Person of the Only-begotten humanity and divinity have been joined, human things become divine and what was man's become God's, "by means of the exchange and unconfused coinherence of each in the other."[133] Nor, as evidenced in the experience of the Apostles on Mt. Thabor, is this deification and the glory revealed in it limited to the Person of Christ alone. Through Christ, it is open to all who believe:

> ...Prayer is the manifestation of divine glory. For when we shut off our sense impressions and draw near to ourselves and to God, and, freed from the commerce of the world outside, enter within ourselves, then we shall see, clearly, the Kingdom of God within ourselves...[134]

"This," he says later echoing the phrase from I Corinthians 2:9 so dear to Symeon, "is what eye has not seen, nor ear heard, nor the heart of man conceived."[135] In these lines the New Theologian could not but have heard the very expression of his own experience.

---

131 Text taken from Vol. V of *Johannes von Damaskos, Die Schriften*, ed. by B. Kotter, (Berlin: 1988), 436-451..

132 *In Trans*. 2.32-35, 438;

133 Ibid. 2.47-49.

134 Ibid. 10.17-20, 448.

135 Ibid. 15.12-13, 453.

Glory and light, and the possibility of experiencing these things in the grace of the Holy Spirit, are nothing new in Greek patristic literature. Symeon is entirely justified in his claim that he is no innovator. He is merely another witness, as he rightly insists, to the tradition which holds that, through the resurrection of Christ and the gift of the Spirit, the Kingdom of God is present now, and likewise available now to all who would seek it. We begin the life everlasting in this life. The experience, to be sure, is only partial (*metrios*, as Symeon remarks),[136] but true nonetheless, while "there" it will be full or better, ever more and more complete, an endless increase. These affirmations are as old as Christianity. Mysticism is as much a feature of St Paul as it is of the New Theologian. That which defines Symeon as a Christian mystic, however, as opposed to one of the many in many religions who have spoken about contact with the transcendent, even of the transcendent as light,[137] remains to be stated clearly. We would see it in St Symeon's insistence that this encounter is:

A Personal and Sacramental Experience

The Problem

"It is not possible," writes Symeon, "to know God any other way than through contemplation of the light which is sent out from Him...God is light and the vision of Him is as light."[138] Some might well think it possible, however, to define this experience in impersonal terms. Here we arrive at the rather ambiguous associations with the term "mysticism" which are frequent in modern English. The categories of experience associated with it, such as "oneness," "unity," "union," or as here, "light," can and often are taken as referring to an inherent or natural capacity, a fundamental

---

136 See *ED* X.820, and Darrouzès, *SC* 51, 129, 318-319, note 1, acknowledging
   Symeon's admission that grace is not always consciously perceived.

137 For "light mysticism" in comparative religion, see M. Eliade *The Two
   and the One* (New York: 1962), 19-77.

138 *ED* V.255-276.

identity between the thing (deity, God, etc.) experienced and the one who experiences it, very much akin to the phrase, "Thou art That," from the Hindu *Upanishads*.[139] We can, moreover, easily find analogues to the mysticism of the Orient in the Greco-Roman world of late antiquity which comprised the patrimony of any educated Byzantine (which category includes the fathers of the Church). In particular, the writings of the Neo-platonist philosophers present us with an understanding of the encounter with divinity which recalls the Hindu phrase just quoted. The Neo-platonists spoke of union with God as a "return to the self."[140] Reality, *the* reality which underlies the phenomenal world and in the last analysis makes of the latter a shadow realm, a kind of "theater" analogous to the Hindu *maya*,[141] is identical with the deep self, again comparable to the Hindu *atman*. The goal of the wise man is therefore, according to the formula of the greatest of the pagan Neoplatonists, the "flight of the alone to the alone."[142] It is also true that we find this same phrase, in these words and in many variations, repeated throughout Symeon's own writings.[143] How then can we maintain that the New Theologian, precisely as mystic, does not depart from Christianity's insistence on the transcendent God, on salvation as accomplished in the person of Christ and as mediated through the Church and, in particular, the Church's sacraments?

---

139 From the Chandogya Upanishad, in *The Upanishads*, trans. and selected by J. Mancaro, (1966), 117-118.

140 See, for example, Plotinus, *Enneads* V.1.11 (Loeb, 49-50), VI.5.7 (Loeb, 338-340), and E. Brehier, *The Philosophy of Plotinus* (Chicago: 1958), esp. 182-194.

141 See p. 70, note 75 above.

142 Plotinus, *Enn* VI.7.34 (Loeb, 190, line 8). There are, however, some hesitations on Plotinus' part regarding the strict identity of the One with the many. His is far from an unqualified monism, and the word itself is perhaps debatable with respect to his thought. Compare *Enn* II.9.3, V.1.6, and V.4.1 with the suggestion of the One as creator in VI.*8.19*. See also the article by A.H. Armstrong, "The Escape of the One," *SP* 13 (1973): 77-89.

143 See, for example, *H* 23.2 and 23.425-429 (M, 113 and 122), and 27.70-79 (M, 143-144).

Symeon would certainly have been in good company. Such attitudes were nothing new in the Christian East. From the gnostic movement through Origen and Evagrius to Messalianism and the various dualisms active in the Empire—Manichees, Paulicians, Bogomils—both before and during Symeon's lifetime, one can find a persistent indifference, or even hostility, to both the personal and historical concreteness of Jesus Christ, and the institutions of the Church. How is Symeon's mysticism not reducible to a metaphysic which boils down in turn, in however qualified a version, to monism? Is he or is he not an advocate of the reality of created existence which, while open to God, is still other than the Creator?

Person to Person: A Fervent Devotion to Christ

We begin the reply by repeating our assertion above. Symeon was a Christian and convinced that the world perceived by the senses is not a "theater" of meaningless activity. It is rather the arena of ultimate concerns, of the ascetic ordeal, of the encounter with Christ in one's brother. He is attached in the deepest way to the person of Jesus, and his mysticism is not confined, as Archbishop Basil rightly notes, to the vision of light in general:

> ...it is often said that the mysticism of the Greek Fathers is a mysticism of light...[which] marks the highest aspirations of Byzantine spirituality. At least in the case of Symeon, such a view can only be accepted with reservations. For him it is not the vision of light as such...that constitutes the central moment...but rather a personal encounter with Christ manifesting Himself through light... A simple vision of light does not bestow this.[144]

From this personal meeting with the person of the Word all the rest flows: Church, sacraments, creation redeemed in and transfigured by-yet never simply identical to-the Word enfleshed.

144 Krivocheine, *Light*, 22.

Symeon's experience of union is therefore always to be understood as a cleaving to someone else, to Christ. One might perhaps raise against him the accusation of an impersonal and abstract, hence debatably Christian, mysticism had his experiences been confined simply to something like "George's" ecstasy in the light. Yet we have seen that they were not. He himself notes that the young man's rapture was not rooted in the solid foundation of ascetic practice,[145] and that its effect quickly dissipated as a result. It is rather as a monk, following the discipline of his elder, that he grows in the knowledge of God until finally he meets and converses with Christ. His experience comes for him as the confirmation of the Christian tradition.

Christ has often appeared in our quotations from Symeon's works. The Lord who comes to him and Whom he loves is not a symbol or cipher for some supra-personal experience, but the Jesus of the Gospels. References, frequent and intense, to Christ's passion abound in his works. In the first chapter of *Discourse* II, for example, where he takes up arms against those who claim predestination as an excuse for lack of effort, his first and heartfelt weapon is an appeal to Christ's suffering and death. The Lord, he tells his interlocutors, died for you alone, and you were bought with the price of His blood.[146] The cross is something immediate and personal for Symeon which he expects his listeners to feel as well. Indeed, the whole argument of *Discourse* II, essentially an appeal to the salvation history, is designed to elicit the twin response of faith and love. All things, from the creation of Eve to the Incarnation, have been subject to God's plan to save all and each. Moreover, Christ's cross is the example set before every believer.[147] We

145 *C* 22.246-329 (dec, 250-252).
146 *ED* II.1.159-166.
147 *C* 5.311-339 (deC, 98-99).

are all to imitate Christ's sufferings.[148] It is Jesus' own love for humanity in *Catechesis* 1, which is the new Zion not made with hands, our true dwelling and eternal city.[149] The Lord's commandments are not instructions in morality but, as we saw above, instead "sacramental" in nature, i.e., in observing them we are led to communion with Him "Who is hidden within His divine commandments."[150]

Everything in the New Theologian's thinking is aimed at coming into personal contact with the Lord Jesus. Christ's activity within us, at first unknown and unperceived in the early stages of Christian life,[151] takes place in order that, finally, He may

> ... reveal Himself openly to us, as faithful and obedient,
> as true disciples and friends, just as of old He revealed
> Himself to His disciples and apostles ...then we become
> sons of God by grace.[152]

Symeon's *Hymns* are frequently couched in the form of a dialogue. Always he is aware that he is speaking with Another, with the Friend and the Beloved. It is Jesus Who visits him "while I am sitting on my bed...within my cell,"[153] and Who ravishes him with wonder and astonishment:

> O the miracle! I find Him abiding
> and moving, and speaking within me,
> and He renders me altogether speechless
> with astonishment at His unapproachable glory.[154]

---

148 *C* 28.262-291 (deC, 302-303). The passage, as in his *Letter on Confession*, bears on the authority to forgive sins as not limited to the ordained.

149 *C* 1.53-69 (deC, 42-43).

150 *ED* VI.102-107.

151 See *Ch* III.76-77 (*SC* 51, 104; McG, 74-75), and J. Darrouzès, note 1: "Syméon donc admet une action de Dieu et même l'enseignement dont nous n'avons pas conscience; on voit par là combien il faut nuancer sa pensée avec doigté," i.e., Symeon does admit of grace which works in the Christian unperceived.

152 *Ch* III.77 (*SC* 51, 104; McG, 74-74).

153 *H* 13.63-66 (M, 45).

154 *H* 20.33-36 (M, 89).

He knows that he will never be alone, "for how can the bride be separated from the Bridegroom,"[155] and is continually astounded at the paradox "that I see Him Who holds all things in the palm of His hand contained within my heart."[156] He knows Who it is Who has lifted him up, clothed him with grace, and made him the "throne of Your divinity and home of Your unapproachable glory and kingdom."[157] He, Symeon, is the throne, house, vessel, and candle stand. That which the throne bears, the house and vessel contain, and which burns on the candle stand is Another.

Paradox is the key here, and in the tensions of that paradox we may discern the fundamentally Christian nature of Symeon's mysticism. He is always fully aware that he, a thing of clay, is incapable of receiving his Maker. His self, his "alone," can never be thus identified with the "Alone" which is God. Between the two "alones" the gap is absolute and unbridgeable. Yet in Christ, and using language taken from the long tradition of patristic thought concerning the union of God and man in Jesus (to which we shall turn below), he recognizes that this gap has been bridged-miraculously, inexplicably, mysteriously, but still bridged and joined. This is the work of divine grace which is offered to humanity and which, on our accepting it, makes us "gods" by adoption. Again, there is nothing impersonal here, no simple realization of potentialities inherent in the human being, but instead the activity and mercy of the Other. As Christ says to Symeon in *Catechesis* 34:

> I am the kingdom of God that is hidden in your midst... though by nature I cannot be contained, yet even here below I am contained in you by grace; though I am invisible I become visible...I am the leaven the soul receives... [I am] He Who takes the place of the visible

155 *H* 27.49 [AK, 48], (M, 143).
156 *H* 20.38-39 (M, 90).
157 Ibid. 196-203 (M, 93).

> Paradise and becomes a spiritual paradise for My ser-
> vants...I am the sun Who rises in them every hour as in
> the morning and am seen by the intellect, just as I in
> times past manifested Myself in the prophets...[158]

Time and again he returns to this paradox. It is the very core of his experience that he who is "straw may partake of fire" and be "refreshed with dew, beyond all speech. . .as in olden times the bush burning with fire was unconsumed."[159] He knows that "human nature is incapable of bearing" the clear vision of God, yet

> ...we believe that we receive You entire, O my Christ,
> from the Spirit Whom You give [us], O my God,
> And we confess that in communing
> of Your spotless blood and flesh
> We take hold of You and eat You,
> O God, without division or confusion...
> You impart to me your own incorruptible
> purity, O Word, and make me light
> who before was darkness...[160]

A Sacramental Mysticism and a Real Presence

The reference to the Eucharist above brings us to the question of Symeon's reverence for the sacraments. The paradox of an infinite God contained in a finite and mortal body for him is realized again and perhaps pre-eminently in the sacraments of Baptism and, especially, the Eucharist. This is especially evident in, for example, *Discourse* III. Here it is clear that he feels no conflict between his devotion to and encounter with Christ "in the heart" and the Lord's presence in the consecrated elements on the altar. Communion with Christ in the heart and at the altar are reciprocal. Better, they are one and the same mystery. Thus, having completed his analysis of II

158 *C* 32.309-337 (deC, 356).

159 From the prayer, ascribed to St Symeon, in preparation for Holy Communion, *A Manual of Eastern Orthodox Prayers* (Crestwood: 1983), 74.

160 *H* 20.14-27 (M, 89).

Corinthians 12, he turns and asks his readers: "Do you want me
to tell you what the good things are which eye has not seen nor
ear heard...?" and answers his question with:

> These...eternal good things...which God has prepared
> for those who love Him, are not protected by heights,
> nor enclosed in some secret place...They are right in
> front of you, before your very eyes...[they] are the Body
> and Blood of our Lord Jesus Christ which we see every
> day, and eat, and drink...[161]

The kingdom of God, the blessings of heaven and society of
Christ are communicated to the believer in and through the
physical elements. This is nothing more than the extension or
continuation of the Incarnation. The Uncontainable was/is contained in a mortal frame and so, now, He comes to us in the
bread and wine. It is the same Christ, and we partake of the same
flesh in the Eucharist that was taken from Mary the Virgin and
indissolubly wedded to the Creator Word.[162] Bread and wine
become the vehicles and presence of the world to come.

Yet, as Symeon points out, quoting from John 6 in the same
discourse, the unbelieving Jews also met the incarnate Word.
But they failed to discern the glory veiled in His humanity.
Their lack of faith blinded them, and Jesus thus appeared to
them as merely another man. The same principle, he argues,
applies to the reception of the Eucharist. Whoever partakes
must "see this bread with spiritual eyes, and see that this little
particle is made divine." Otherwise, one fails to "eat the heavenly bread, but [consumes] only the earthly bread, and
thus...[is] deprived of life."[163] He therefore warns his readers:

> So then, you must not be like the Jews as well, mutter-
> ing and saying: 'Is this not the bread on the diskos and
> the wine in the chalice which we see every day...? How

161 *ED* III.426-435.
162 *ED* I.10.166-175.
163 *ED* III.535-536.

does this man say that these are the good things which
eye has not seen, nor ear heard...?'[164]

The mystery of Christ's presence is discerned "with spiritual
eyes," without which the Eucharist "looks like any fragment of
bread."[165]

Does this mean that Symeon sees the grace of the sacraments as essentially a "subjective" reality, or that the presence
of Christ in them is less than "objective?" Some critics have
certainly argued that this is the case, seeing in him either the
herald of Protestant personalism[166] or else tinged with "Messalianism."[167] Their difficulty is related to the problem we
discussed above concerning the New Theologian's understanding of confession and the authority to absolve, and just as
clearly it derives, at least in good part, from the same inability
to confront him on his own terms and in his own context, i.e.,
apart from the Reformation-Counter Reformation battle over
the place and meaning of the sacraments.

The difficulty stems, again, from the tension in his thought
between what one scholar calls the "ecclesiastical position"
and "mystical individualism,"[168] or as we put it above, between
institution and charism. Symeon means first of all that the
sacraments are not truly efficacious without the perception
which is granted through the activity of the Holy Spirit:

It is the Spirit Who is really the true food and drink. It
is the Spirit Who changes the bread into the Lord's
body. It is the Spirit Who really purifies us and makes
us partake worthily of the body of the Lord.[169]

164 Ibid. 456-60.
165 *ED* XIV.257-258.
166 Holl, 98.
167 See esp. Miguel, "Conscience de la grâce," 385, and Darrouzès (*SC*
129, 282, note 2) complaining of the lack of an *ex opere operato* in
Symeon.
168 Völker, *Praxis*, 187.
169 *ED* III.547-549. The statement, "It is the Spirit Who changes the

The sacraments are thus truly "spiritual" in nature and the "real presence" of Christ in them likewise "spiritual." The difficulty here is the modern confusion which opposes spiritual to physical, equates it in effect with the dichotomy between mind and matter. This is not Symeon's point at all. He is not advocating a distinction which goes back to Plato. Rather, he is insisting on the eschatological nature of the Church. This is clearly the case in the following from the tenth chapter of *Discourse* I:

> ...it is by means of this [flesh] that He Who is Son of God and Son of the Virgin communicates the grace of the Spiriti.—i.e., of divinity—from, on the one hand, the nature and essence of His co-eternal Father, as He says Himself through His prophet: "And it will come to pass that in those days I will pour out My Spirit upon all flesh" [Joel 2:28]—on all flesh, clearly that believes—and, on the other hand, from the flesh which He took from her...[170]

The citation from the prophecy of Joel concerning the "last days" is crucial. Symeon's central point in the whole discourse is that the Church, as the Body of Christ risen from the dead and quickened by the Spirit, is the new creation, the new world. Extending his argument to the Eucharist, he can therefore say that unless one lives in the Spirit and is fully and consciously a citizen of the "New Jerusalem," one eats and drinks "mere" bread and wine in the same way that the Jews of John 6 saw Jesus as "merely" another man.

Everything turns around the parallel between Christ before the Jews and the Eucharist as "received" by people who are, in effect, unbelievers. Given this parallel, one cannot seriously argue that the divine presence in the consecrated gifts is for

bread," refers to the *epiclesis* or invocation of the Holy Spirit which, in the Byzantine and other Eastern liturgies, follows the "Words of Institution" and is believed to complete the consecration of the elements.

170 *ED* I.10.129-137.

Symeon anything less than "real." The Eucharist is the presence of that same body born of Mary and now, through the Resurrection, entirely "spiritualized," i.e., moved and quickened by the Holy Spirit. The New Testament accounts of Christ's Resurrection tell, after all, of a change, not of a simple resuscitation.[171] Although in continuity with the flesh and blood of the son of Mary who walked in Palestine, Christ's body is likewise changed. Symeon is fully aware of this and, in a significant passage from *Hymn* 26, he links the Eucharist to the "altered state" which Christ demonstrates in His post-Resurrection appearances to the disciples:

> You deify Your sensible body and blood
> and alter them without change into what is neither held nor grasped,
> rather in truth You transform them into what is spiritual, invisible.
> Just as of old You came and left through doors which were shut
> and [at another time] became invisible to the eyes
> of Your disciples at the breaking of the bread,
> so now do You consecrate this bread and make it Your spiritual body.[172]

The thought is fully biblical and equally removed from either a crude "physicalism" regarding the sacrament, "You did not," says Symeon a little later, "become man in order to remain in our heaviness and be held by corruption,"[173] or the simple equation of "spiritual" with immaterial. The Eucharist is the

171 See, for example, I Cor. 15:42-54 and, from the gospels, Jn 20:11-19 and Lk 24:13-31, as well the studies by J.A.T. Robinson, *The Body: A Study in Pauline Theology*, (Philadelphia: 1952), 49-83; F.X. Durrwell, *The Resurrection: A Biblical Study*, trans. by R. Sheed, (New York: 1960), 108-150; and V. Kesich, *The First Day of the New Creation*, (Crestwood: 1982), 127-153.

172 *H* 26.43-50 (M, 140).

173 Ibid. 62-63.

flesh and blood of the historical Jesus, but it is flesh and blood transformed into what is "spiritual and invisible," the new reality of the world to come.

And it is real. Whether the recipient perceives it or not, that reality is present in the sacrament. In *Hymn* 58, Symeon speaks in the person of Christ condemning those of His bishops

> Who think indeed that they hold bread, which in fact is fire,
> and hold Me in contempt as merely bread,
> and fancy that they see and eat a particle of bread
> without perceiving My invisible glory. [174]

Such people, he continues, are laying up for themselves a terrible condemnation. They are like Judas who betrayed his Master because they fail to discern Who He is and mistake Him for what He is not. The bread of the Eucharist is never "ordinary." [175] In the same vein he writes elsewhere of his dread and wonder at having been made worthy of "becoming ...celebrant of the divine mysteries and minister of the spotless Trinity." "For," he adds,

> whenever the bread is set down and the wine poured out...there are You Yourself, my God and Word, and these things truly become Your body and blood by the descent of the Spirit; and daring to approach them, we touch the unapproachable God. [176]

It is a sentiment often expressed in his works that Christ gives what is "really (*ousiodos*, literally, essentially)" His flesh, and that the blood which we drink is the same as that "which was poured out: for my sake You were slaughtered." [177] Christ not only speaks within the heart of this mystic, but gives Himself as food and drink. [178]

---

174 *H* 58.93-96 (M, 290).
175 Ibid. 123ff; cf also *ED* III.590ff.
176 *H* 14.52-60 (M, 48).
177 *H* 20.58-61 (M, 90).
178 Cf. Völker, *Praxis*, 409 (referring to H 20), and Krivocheine, *Light,* 122.

The same realism holds as well for Symeon's understanding of Baptism. He links the two sacraments together during the course of his attack in *Discourse* IX on his favorite targets, the professional theologians:

> Brothers, if the full knowledge of the true wisdom and knowledge of God were going to be given us through letters and formal study, what need would there be then for faith, or for divine Baptism, or even communion in the Mysteries? Obviously, none whatever.[179]

Yet, here again certain aspects of his thought have given rise to questions, particularly his references to-and apparent preference for-the "second Baptism" of tears. Some see in this emphasis, which admittedly is of considerable importance for Symeon, the signs of anything from a tenth-century anticipation of twentieth-century American Pentecostalism[180] to a "characteristic tension...according to which [personal] enlightenment is decisive [while] the sacramental proceedings are not so to the same degree."[181] Symeon would seem to be supporting the second assertion in a passage like the following:

> The first Baptism has the water which foreshadows the tears, [and] it has the *myron* of the anointing which signifies beforehand the intelligible *myron* of the Spirit. The second [Baptism], however, is no longer a type of the truth, but is the truth itself.[182]

It is through these tears, the fruit of repentance and the stirrings of the Spirit within, that "one is purified and baptized with the second baptism."[183]

179 *ED* IX.10-15.
180 Maloney, *Fire and Light*, has something of this emphasis, though not without qualifications. See 10ff on the need in Symeon's day for a "new Pentecost" in the Byzantine Church, but see also 134ff for warnings against a too easy comparison with modern Pentecostalism.
181 Völker, *Praxis*, 183.
182 *Ch* I.36 (*SC* 51, 50; McG, 42).
183 Ibid. I.35.

The notion of a "baptism of tears" was long-established in the monastic and pre-monastic tradition,[184] and Symeon is certainly taking up here from Step 7 of John of Sinai's *Ladder* as well as from Isaac of Syria. But is he, as the two passages above seem to indicate, also maintaining that the first baptism functions merely as a kind of sign pointing toward the necessity of a personal and conscious experience? If so, then one would be justified in seeing him as the harbinger of that rejection of sacramentalism characteristic of the more radical reformers. It is not, however, a genuine axiom of Symeon's that "all grace, in order to be active in people, must be consciously appropriated."[185] He may come at times perilously close to this, but he never quite falls over the edge. In the same set of *Theological and Practical Chapters* we quoted from just now, he also speaks of those things which "God has taught and commanded us secretly and in ways we are not aware of."[186] God does, for him, work in us when we are not consciously aware of Him. And, of all the ways in which He acts thus, Baptism is the most important:

> We have been baptized as babies, unaware,
> As incomplete we also incompletely received the grace,
> receiving the remission from the first transgression.[187]

The grace is incomplete here in the sense that it requires completion through actively chosen appropriation, i.e., the way of the virtues. But, for all that, it is still grace, and it is essential. What Adam lost in Eden is regained. This is first of all freedom from slavery to the devil, the power to do good:

---

184 See the article by S. Mary, "St Symeon the New Theologian and the Way of Tears," *SP* 10 (1970): 431-435, as well as Völker, 197-200, and Krivocheine, *Light*, 141-148. For "tears" in the Eastern tradition, see M. Lot-Borodine, "Le mystère des larmes," *Vie Spirituelle* (1936), 65-110, and for a rich selection of original texts, I. Hausherr, *Penthos*, 123-136.

185 Holl, 53.

186 *Ch* III.77 (*SC* 51, 103; McG, 95), and see page 105, note 136 above.

187 *H* 55.38-40 (M, 280).

...we have been born again in holy Baptism and have
been released from slavery and become free, so that the
enemy cannot take any action against us unless we of
our own will obey him...[188]

This is no small thing. Baptism removes the "ancestral sin,"[189]
and more. Through it we receive power not only to do good,
but "to be called sons of God and be clothed upon with
Christ."[190] Baptism, Symeon continues in *Hymn 55*, replaces
us in paradise, engrafts us into the vine of Christ.[191]

However, this real power can be lost. The grace and indwelling of the Spirit, to use Symeon's own image, can "leak
away" if there is no effort to put this new freedom to the
purpose for which it was given.[192] And that, of course, is what
happens inevitably to everyone who lives past infancy. Thus
all are in need of repentance and the baptism of tears, tears as
sign both of fervent contrition and of the operation of the Spirit.
It may be true thus to speak of the grace in sacramental Baptism
as "one and the same" in Symeon with that of the Holy Spirit
in the tears and light which mark the "second" baptism.[193]
Certainly, it is the same Spirit at work in both and, moreover,
the view that all grace is pre-contained, as it were, in this
sacrament is well-established in the tradition of spiritual literature familiar to the New Theologian.[194] But this forthright and

188 *C* 5.445-448 (deC, 101-102).

189 The traditional phrase in the East for what Western Christianity calls
"original sin." For the eastern understanding, see J. Romanides, *To
Propaterikon Hamartema*, 2d ed, (Athens: 1989), and in English, J.
Meyendorff, *Byzantine Theology*, 143-146.

190 *C* 24.172-176 (deC, 165).

191 *H* 55.43-51 (M, 280).

192 Ibid. 55.2ff (M, 279); see also *C* 27.67-98 (deC, 286), and *ED* XIV.267-
274.

193 Van Rossum, "Priesthood," 223; see also H.M. Biedermann, *Das Menschenbild bei Symeon dem Jüngeren, dem Theologen* (Würzburg,
1949), 158.

194 See our reference on page 72, note 85 above. Note as well Maximus

direct equation makes Symeon perhaps more simple than in fact he is. He does evidence a certain "oscillation" between the two poles, institutional/charismatic, objective/subjective, which characterize his thought and his inheritance. The grace of Baptism is real indeed, but only a "type" if it is not fulfilled, i.e., brought to fruition, just as the Eucharist is "mere" bread if not perceived in the Spirit; or Christ "mere" man if not seen with the eyes of faith. Such "failed grace" brings the greater condemnation. No merely "objective" presence can bring about anyone's salvation for Symeon, not even the "objective" presence of the Word of God Himself. Response is called for on the part of a willing subject, the created person replying to the uncreated God in Trinity. And this leads us to his thought concerning God and man.

Confessor, *Centuries on Charity* IV.69 and 77 (*PG* 90.1064D-1065A and 1068A; Eng. in *Philokalia* II, ed. by Ware et. al., 109-110).

The Theologian

St Symeon is both heir and contributor—he would probably have preferred the term "witness"—to the patrimony of the Greek Fathers. Yet, while he doubtless would have seen himself as simply passing on the substance of truths inherited from the Church's tradition and confirmed by his experience, the actions of receiving and then transmitting a tradition are never so simple. A great twentieth-century Orthodox theologian pointed out some years ago that a truly patristic theology is never a matter of simply repeating the great saints and teachers of the past, but requires instead acquiring the "mind of the Fathers."[1] Another, contemporary scholar has underlined the difference between the mechanical—hence, inevitably distorting—repetition of ancient truths and their creative and living appropriation with the aphorism, "tradition is the living faith of the dead, traditionalism the dead faith of the living."[2] As we have seen, Symeon was in his own day confronted with a species of the latter, a desire to freeze the past in place and surround it with an impenetrable, golden aura. This desire is universally human, but it was particularly powerful in the conservatism which marked Byzantine society throughout its history, and most especially the Church authorities of the eleventh to thirteenth centuries. Such a posture was bound to come into conflict with someone whose whole being was in the service of the Gospel proclamation that the Kingdom of God

1 Georges Florovsky. See his "Gregory Palamas and the Church of the Fathers," in *Bible, Church, Tradition*, vol. I, *The Collected Works* (Belmont, Massachusetts: 1972), 107-112.

2 Jaroslav Pelikan, *Emergence of the Catholic Tradition: 100-600*, (Chicago: 1971), 9.

is truly and literally "at hand." Symeon's pathos, his glory and his cross, lay in his steadfast affirmation that to place any barrier whatever, be it out of motives of conventional piety or timid complacency, between the Apostles and saints of old and the Christians of his own day counted as blasphemy, the "heresy of pusillanimity," he calls it in *Catechesis* 29.[3] Nothing was so fixed in him as his conviction that the tradition is like a living current that passes from one generation to another as electricity flows through a wire, or—and these are his words—as fire is transferred from one kindled lamp to another.[4] It is, in short, as personal encounter and transformation that he understands the content of the Church's theology. The latter's dogmas are the echo in words of the impossible experience of the transcendent Word made flesh. These words have been stretched and hammered over the generations into a shape which conforms as closely as humanly possible to that experience. Symeon's own language, accordingly, creaks and pops on occasion under the strain of its burden. Not surprisingly, in any such appropriation of what for his adversaries were revered and sacrosanct *formulae*, he is occasionally led to statements which at first blush, like some of those we met above concerning the sacraments, appear to transgress or at least to play dangerously around the edges of the canons of received Orthodoxy. But it is precisely here that Symeon lays the groundwork for the further adaptation of language to the demands of the Christian mystery. Much of his work will be carried on in particular by St Gregory Palamas three centuries later, and there is not a little left over for those of our own and subsequent ages to ponder.

---

3   *C* 29. It is the title of the *Discourse*. For description of the "heresy," see the same, 29.137-167 (deC, 312), and also *C* 32.1-58 (deC, 335-336).

4   See *ED* VIII.249-259; see also VII.509-556.

Of the Holy Trinity

It is appropriate that we begin here, not only because the Trinity is the heart of the Christian Gospel, but also because it is concerning the Trinity that we have the one and only theological question that we can be certain was ever asked the New Theologian: Stephen of Nicomedia's request that he reply to the question whether the three Persons are distinguishable only in theory (*epinoiai*) or in fact (*pragmati*). We saw above that he passed this test with flying colors, and nowhere do we find that it was ever raised again. Still, one might justly wonder why Stephen asked that particular question. Nicetas ascribes it, of course, entirely to the chancellor's malice,[5] but if we assume that there was more to Stephen than the simple caricature of villainy Nicetas chooses to give us (in accordance with the canons of conventional hagiography that he was following,[6]) then there may well have been more to his question as well. Some of Symeon's remarks or preaching on the Trinity and the mystical life had possibly come back to the chancellor in ways that genuinely troubled him—and, to be sure, which seemed to provide him with a welcome opportunity to bring this troublesome abbot down a peg or two in popular esteem. What is there, then, about Symeon's teaching on the Trinity which could have worried the Church authorities?

Here we must turn to a brief discussion of the Latin and Greek approaches to the Trinity against the background of Church history and politics—in particular the increasing tension between the Churches of West and East—that characterized Symeon's and the chancellor's time. The theology of the Greek fathers lays primary emphasis on the three divine

5   *Vie* 74, (100-102).

6   See Hausherr, *Vie*, xxiff, and Holl, 7ff. Holl, however, is careful to note the exceptional quality of Nicetas' composition, even to the extent of comparing it with St Athanasius' *Life of Antony*.

persons.[7] So great was this insistence by the great Cappadocian
fathers in the fourth century that one of them, Gregory of
Nyssa, was obliged to write a little treatise explaining *Why
there are not three Gods.*[8] The key lay in the word chosen to
denote the Persons, *hypostasis*, originally and intentionally a
much stronger term than the Greek word which was in fact the
exact equivalent of the Latin *persona* (and our "person"),
prosopon. While the two words, *hypostasis* and *prosopon*,
were eventually to acquire the same meaning in Greek theology, this was only because the second was assimilated to the
strong sense of the first.[9] *Hypostasis* had enjoyed a long and
interesting evolution as a philosophical and theological term,[10]
but it always carried with it some of its original force, a force
which we might summarize by noting that it, too, has its more or
less exact Latin equivalent, *substantia*, our word "substance."

This expression was never especially welcome in the Latin
West, and understandably. To Latin ears it sounded as if the

7   There are many modern works on this question. Some of the most useful
    are: V. Lossky, *The Mystical Theology of the Eastern Church,* (London:
    1968, rep.), 44-66; as well as his *Introduction to Orthodox Theology,*
    trans. by Kesarechi-Watson, (Crestwood: 1978), esp. 36-49. See also
    Meyendorff, *Byzantine Theology*, 180-189, together with the standard
    works by J.N.D. Kelly, *Early Christian Doctrines*, 2d ed., (New York:
    1960), 83-137 and 152-179; and G.L. Prestige, *God in Patristic Thought*,
    (London: 1969 rep.): 157-281. The emphasis on the three Hypostases goes
    back to the Cappadocians' admired—if flawed—master, Origen. See the
    latter's *De Principiis*, esp. I.1-3 (SC 252, 90-96; Eng. Butterworth, *On
    First Principles*, [New York: 1966], 7-39).

8   *Gregorii Nysseni Opera*, ed. F. Mueller, III.1, 37-57 (*PG* 45.116-136).
    For English, see *Christology of the Later Fathers*, ed. E.R. Hardy,
    (Philadelphia: 1954), 256-267.

9   For the difficulties, see Prestige, and C. Stead, *Divine Substance*,
    (Oxford: 1979). For the equation of the two terms, see John of Damas-
    cus, *Exp. fid.* 59.156ff (Kotter, v. II, 150), and his *Dialektika* 26/44, ed.
    by Papazere, (Athens: 1978), 118-119.

10 Cf. H. Dörries, "Hypostasis: Wort- und Bedeutungsgeschichte,"
    Nachrichten der Akademie der Wissenschafter in Göttingen (1955),
    35-98.

Greeks were talking about three divine substances, i.e. precisely three gods, and this objection was particularly deeply
rooted in that their theological vocabulary had settled on the
word *substantia* to denote the divine unity since the time of
Tertullian at the turn of the third century.[11] Bishop Dionysius
of Rome had protested the use of *hypostasis* by his namesake
in Alexandria in the mid-third century.[12] Jerome complained
bitterly about the word in a letter a hundred years later to
Dionysius' successor at Rome, Pope Damasus.[13] Augustine of
Hippo never accepted it and, although he rather grudgingly
admitted the term *persona* as sanctioned by the ecclesiastical
tradition,[14] he preferred to turn back to older models of the
Trinity for his inspiration. He liked the "economic" model of
the Trinity favored by St Irenaeus of Lyons, among others,
which was characterized by the notion of an analogy obtaining
between God and His created image, the individual human
being.[15] As image of God, every human being carries the
"footprints of the Trinity (*vestigia trinitatis*)." For Augustine,
the image is located particularly in the human soul or mind, and
consequently it is the soul which presents him with the one
adequate—or least inadequate, since he was not insensitive to
God's transcendence[16]—analogue to the divine mystery.[17]
Hence the predominance in his theology of what is called the

11 See his *Adv. Prax.* 2 and ff (*PL* 2.156B-196C; Eng. *ANF* III, 598ff).

12 See his "Epistle to Dionysius [of Rome]," in *The Letters and Other
    Remains of Dionysius of Alexandria*, ed. C.L. Feltoe, (Cambridge:
    1904); Eng., *ANF* VI, 92-94.

13 *Epistle* 15, *PL* 13.180B-185B; Eng., *Early Latin Theology*, ed. by
    Greenslade, (Philadelphia: 1956), 302-311.

14 *De.trin.* V.9-10, *PL* 42.916-918; Eng., *St Augustine, The Trinity*, trans.
    by E. Hill, (Brooklyn: 1990), 195-196.

15 See for example, *Adv.Haer.* IV, Preface 4, for Son and Spirit as the
    "hands" of the Father (*SC* 100, pt.2, 390; and *ANF* I, 463). For the
    earlier "Logos theology" of Justin Martyr, see Kelly, 96-108.

16 See *De trin.* XV.20-24; *PL* 42.1089-1090; *The Trinity*, 409-416.

17 See *Civ.Dei* XI.xxvi.23-26; *PL* 41.339-340; Eng., in *NPNF* (first se-
    ries) II, 220-222.

psychological model of the Trinity. He is particularly fond, for
example, of the triad, memory-intelligence-will, in the human
soul as a likeness of the relations and co-inherence obtaining
in the divine triad.[18] Given this image as the primary model of the
Trinity, the West's later addition of the phrase *filioque* ("and from
the Son") to the section of the Nicene Creed dealing with the
procession of the Holy Spirit followed naturally. The will in
human beings flows from both memory and intelligence as from
one source. One cannot have it otherwise. Augustine's model not
only allows for, but demands the *filioque* and, given that the
bishop of Hippo would become the *fons et origo* of all subsequent
Latin thinking on the subject, this conclusion would hold for the
entire Western Church as well, both then and now.[19]

This leads us back to Greek patristic thought and eventually
to Symeon and Stephen. For the Greeks the *filioque* was a flat
impossibility. The whole struggle of the fourth century debate
on the Trinity, particularly as it was carried on by the Cappadocian fathers, turned around the inadequacy of the psychological
or any other model for the revealed mystery of the Triune God.
An account of God, or the universe, as the human psyche writ
large lay ready to hand in the speculations of earlier and
contemporary pagan Neo-platonism, especially in the works of
thinkers such as Plotinus, his disciple Porphyry, and Iam-
blichus.[20] Yet, it also seems to have been the case that these

18 See *De trin.* X and XIV; *PL* 42.971-984 and 1035-1058; *Trinity*, 286-
    299 and 370-392.

19 For the unique importance of Augustine in the crucial debate over the
    filioque in the ninth century, see R. Haugh, *Photius and the Carol-
    ingians*, (Belmont, Massachusetts: 1973), 15-54. See also the article by
    P. Deseille, "Ho Hagios Augoustinos kai 'to *Filioque*,'" in *He Poreia
    pros ten Orthodoxia* (Athens, 1986), 71-112.

20 For the oscillation in late Neo-platonist thought between the subjective
    and objective, or microcosm and macrocosm, see S. Gersh, *From
    Iamblichus to Erieugena: Studies in the Pseudo-Dionysian Tradition*,
    (Leiden: 1973), esp. 27-120. The same point is made by E.R. Dodds'
    witty—if a little cruel—summation of Proclus' (d. 486) philosophy as

philosophers were, precisely, the inspiration of those thinkers in the Greek Christian community whom the Cappadocians were most at pains to refute.[21] The writings of Basil the Great and Gregory of Nyssa against Eunomius furnish eloquent testimony to their conviction that language (and, by extension, the human mind) can do no more than point toward a reality which transcends it absolutely. Their positive contribution to the theology of the Trinity is thus based on a careful and deliberate balancing of antitheses.[22] The reality of the divine life lies between different sets of contradictory statements which are subject to no logical resolution. No philosophical calculus can ever solve the equation of the Trinity wherein $1 + 1 + 1 = 1$.

This is certainly a reason, perhaps *the* reason, why Greek triadology insists on the term *hypostasis*. It is a word which is absolute, i.e., it indicates that there is nothing further to which the object under investigation can be reduced. Indeed, the root meaning of the word is "sub-stratum," that which lies underneath, the rock-bottom reality of a thing. Significantly, the word which the Greek fathers used to denote that which is common among the three Persons, *ousia* or essence, has the same meaning. It, too, can signify a single existing thing.[23] The result is paradox: God is three "things" and one "thing" simultaneously. St Gregory of Nazianzus, called the Theologian and a favorite source of the New Theologian, compares the Trinity to "three suns" and "one sun." If the effort to contemplate this

"the projected shadow of logic" wherein the "Aristotelian apparatus...is converted into an objectively conceived hierarchy of entities or forces." *The Elements of Theology* (Oxford: 1971, rep.), xxv.

21 See the articles of J. Daniélou, "Orientations actuelles de la recherche de Grégoire de Nysse," *Écriture et culture philosophique*, ed. M. Harl, (Leiden: 1971), 4-17; and esp. "Eunome l'Arièn et l'exégèse néoplatonicienne du Cratyle," *Révue des études grecques* 69 (1956): 412-432.

22 Lossky, *Mystical Theology*, 33-49.

23 See Stead, *Divine Substance*, (Oxford, 1979), 134-156, for the varied sense of the word in late antiquity; and Prestige, 188-196.

paradox proves too much and the mind falls away dizzy, he adds, that is just what is to be expected.[24] The creature can never comprehend the Creator. But the same fathers were obliged, as we noted with Gregory of Nyssa, to offer some explanation for how this paradox could be and to defend themselves against the charge of tritheism. Nyssa's reply, in the treatise mentioned above, offers the following argument. The Three are One, first, because they share a single divine will and activity (*energeia*), secondly because they have an unique source and cause, the Person of the Father, and thirdly because number and division apply only to the sphere of created existence, of things such as we are able to count. God, however, is "no thing," is wholly transcendent to every thing we call "being." A fourth consideration, present in the Cappadocians and later labeled "co-inherence (*perichoresis*),"[25] argues that each of the Three is present in the Others. All Three, as it were, occupy the same "space." The key is the "monarchy" of the Father Who timelessly "begets" the Son and "breathes" the Spirit.[26] The Three are One because their source and cause (*arche* and *aitia*) are one and the same, the *hypostasis* of the Father Who gives His *ousia* to Son and Spirit. The mode of origin of Each is different. The Father is without origin (*anarchos*), the Son begotten (*gennesis*) and the Spirit proceeds (*ekporeusis*). As Gregory the Theologian points out, however, the actual processes in God to which these terms point must remain permanently hidden from the created intellect. They are the mysteries of the hidden life of the Trinity. Neither human language or comprehension can do any more, assisted by the

24 See his *Theological Oration* V.14 and 31-33; *PG* 36.149A and 168-171; Eng., *Christology of the Later Fathers*, 202 and 213-214.

25 For the history of this term, see Prestige, 291-299, and for a different view, V. Harrison, "Perichoresis in the Greek Fathers," *St Vladimir's Theological Quarterly* 35 (1991): 53-65.

26 *Theological Oration* III.2ff; *PG* 36.76Aff; *Later Fathers*, 161ff.

revelation, than indicate their presence. Anything more would comprise an ignorant and illusory trespass on the divine majesty and result, Gregory adds, in madness.[27]

With some fine tuning in the centuries following, this was the "model" of the Trinity inherited by St Symeon and jealously preserved by the Church authorities of his day. It was also clearly different from, and perhaps even antithetical to, the "model" proposed by Augustine and followed by the Latin West. East and West had already clashed over this difference several times before Symeon's birth. As early as the seventh century St Maximus the Confessor had tried to explain (rather inadequately, as it happens) the Latin *filioque* to his fellow Greek speakers.[28] The issue had blown up into a full-scale quarrel in the days of the great Patriarch Photius some eighty years before the New Theologian was born, and that division had only been put to rest by Rome's agreement in 879 not to add to the original Creed.[29] The two different theologies, however, remained intact in their respective centers. Finally, right around the time of Symeon's quarrel with Stephen, the Roman popes quietly added the *filioque* to their official profession of faith and, just as quietly, were dropped as a result from the official diptychs (commemorations) of the Patriarch in Constantinople.[30] It would therefore not be assuming too much if we were to say that, at the turn of the eleventh century, the official watchdogs of Orthodoxy at the patriarchal court were highly sensitive and finely attuned to any possible deviation from the received theology of the Trinity and, especially, to

27 *Theological Oration* V.8; *PG* 36.141; *Later Fathers*, 198-199.

28 *PG* 91.136AB.

29 See F. Dvornik's *The Photian Schism*, (Cambridge: 1970, rep.), 159-201, and Meyendorff, *Byzantine Theology*, 58-61 and 92. Of note is the dialogue between Pope Leo III and the Carolingians over the desirability of placing the *filioque* in the Creed. The Pope refused. See the translation from *PL* 102 in Haugh, 81-88.

30 See S. Runciman, *The Eastern Schism*, (Oxford: 1963 rep.), 28-34.

any suggestion which might lead in the direction of the Latin
filioque.

Still, this does not explain Stephen's questioning Symeon
in particular. Ostensibly, and unquestionably with complete
sincerity and even dogged conviction, the New Theologian
upheld the traditional doctrine of the Greek Church. We have
noted his thorough defeat of Stephen's attempt to entrap him.
Archbishop Basil, for example, describes Symeon's triadology
as "resolutely Orthodox."[31] The same scholar further points
out the New Theologian's insistence on the unknowability of
the trinitarian mystery,[32] his consequent refusal to acknowledge the adequacy of any image for it,[33] and his emphasis on
the names of "Begetter," "Begotten," and "Proceeding" as
indicators beyond which human intelligence cannot pene-
trate[34]—all of which sound familiar notes from Greek patristic
thought. They also, perhaps, indicate Symeon's awareness and
conscious rejection of the Latin *filioque.*

But the story does not end there. Archbishop Basil himself
notes that Symeon has recourse on occasion to the psychological
model to illustrate his experience, and specifically points out his
reference to the union of man with God as comprising a "threefold
hypostasis" with the deified human being as thus an image of the
Trinity.[35] We have observed Symeon's use of the composition of
the human soul as analogy for the Trinity in *Discourse* III. There,
and elsewhere,[36] he resorts to the terms "soul" (*psyche*), "reason" (*logos*), and "intellect" (*nous*). These three function as
one, and are one, and their real unity reflects the Triune God as

31 Krivocheine, *Light*, 277-280.
32 See *ED* IX.19ff.
33 Ibid.
34 *C* 33.176-192 (deC, 344).
35 Krivocheine, *Light*, 288-289, citing *ED* VI.137-178 and *C* 15.72-77
    (deC, 195).
36 See also *H* 23 and 44, and *TD* 2.63ff and 187ff respectively (McG,
    125-130).

the Latter's image. Elsewhere again, in *Discourse* IV, he sees the Trinity reflected in the unified functioning of the three faculties of the soul, the "reason-emotion-appetite" (*logistikon, thymetikon, epithymetikon*), traditional in Eastern ascetic literature from the time of Evagrius:

> When, therefore, appetite is fulfilled by all these good things, then the whole of the emotive faculty is as well wholly mingled with the appetitive and the rational faculties, and the three are one in contemplation of the Threefold Unity... At that point their threefold distinction is no longer discernible, but they are wholly one.[37]

So far as we know this passage is unique in Greek patristic literature. To be fair, it is also unique in Symeon's corpus. He usually prefers the triad noted just above. However, in another remarkable and equally unique passage from *Hymn* 12, he compares the Son and Spirit to eyes in a single face (or person, *prosopon*): "For the Three appear to me like two beautiful eyes filled with light, in a single face."[38] With this image we find ourselves on ground trodden eight hundred years before by Irenaeus of Lyons—territory which is not that far distant, in fact, from the country of Augustine. Finally, one of the images for the Trinity which he specifically rejects, and which was clearly popular with his adversaries, is Gregory of Nazianzus' likening of the Three to three suns:

> ...when they hear of God that in the Trinity there is the light of a single godhead just as there is a single mingling of light among three suns, right away they picture three suns in their imagination, united in the light...and distinguished in the hypostases, and then they stupidly imagine that they see the Trinity itself, and that the holy...Trinity is just like their imagined paradigm.[39]

---

37 *ED* IV.424-429.

38 *H* 12.23-24 (M, 39).

39 *ED* IX.33-40.

Now these passages represent only a small percentage of Symeon's references to the Trinity. Even altogether they scarcely support the argument, advanced by his earliest modern critic, that the New Theologian was fundamentally opposed to the "inherent tritheism of the Greek" and favored instead a trinitarian modalism centered on the divinity of Christ.[40] Even the rejection of Gregory the Theologian's "three suns" just cited must be taken in the context, clear from the quotation itself, that Symeon is arguing against an overly rationalizing and literal confidence in something which, after all, was offered simply as an image and not as a detailed "map" of the godhead. His own dependence on Gregory is in any case too deep and well-documented to need any defense in this essay.[41] He knows the ground too well, and the overwhelming majority of his references to the Trinity are in complete accord with the tradition he inherited and wholeheartedly affirmed.[42]

Nonetheless, it is not so difficult to see how Stephen may have been genuinely troubled (and perhaps a little gleeful) on hearing something like—or taken from—the passages just quoted, and very likely garbled in the process of transmission. We might then see his question as a legitimate one, prompted by a real, if slightly overwrought, concern for the integrity of the faith. But the matter does not stop there, either. It would be too easy and quite wrong to dismiss Symeon's recourse to the psychological model as a passing aberration in an otherwise admirable witness to the tradition. We would be better advised to take it quite seriously. It is, after all, the product of his own experience, and the passages employing the psychological model in, particularly, *Discourse* III are among the most powerful he writes anywhere. Granted, there is in him none of

40 Holl, 104-105. No other critic of Symeon, to our knowledge, has advanced quite so radical a view of his triadology.

41 See Völker, *Praxis*, esp. 355-356.

42 See, for example, *H* 52.21-28, and 11.50-54.

Augustine's sophistication and certainly none of the latter's pro-grammatic rejection of Cappadocian thought (insofar as he was aware of it). Symeon's approach is instead a very rough and ready one. He simply snatches at the vocabulary nearest to hand con-cerning the make-up of the soul. "Intellect," "soul," and "reason" are pretty general stuff. Yet, there are similarities with Augustine. Symeon reaches for the analogy of the soul, almost instinctively, to explain his experience. He wants an "inner" explanation of the Trinity which is based at once on his own experience of himself, hard-won through the tempering of traditional asceticism, and on the gratuitous gift of God's self-revelation. This is not so very different from Augustine. He, too, struggled and was also ac-corded an experience of the divine majesty,[43] and he, too, then turned inward to find the explanation for both.

The triadology of the New Theologian is therefore some-thing of a milestone for Greek patristic thought. His lead was not much followed in the centuries afterward. There are glim-merings in such writers as St Gregory Palamas[44] and perhaps others, but glimmerings they remain. The challenge to follow up on Symeon's lead remains for this generation or for others yet to come. Whether pursuing him here will lead to anything substantial, such as a tentative validation of Augustine's ap-proach or even a solution to the chasm dividing West from East on the Trinity, remains to be seen. We can make no predictions, and certainly no attempt to offer any picture of that solution, if such is possible. Still, we do feel obliged to note that Symeon has perhaps opened a door, a possibility, and that we would surely be remiss if we were to ignore it.

43 See his *Confessions*, IX.x.24-25; PL 32.774-775; Eng. in *NPNF* I, 137-138.

44 See Gregory's *Cap.phys.* 30; *PG* 150.144D-145A; see also D. Staniloae, *Theology and the Church*, trans. by R. Barringer, (Crest-wood: 1980), 11-44, M.E. Hussey, "The Palamite Trinitarian Models," *St Vladimir's Theological Quarterly* 16 (1972): 83-89, and R.E. Sinkiewicz, "Introduction," *St Gregory Palamas: The One Hundred and Fifty Chapters* (Toronto: 1988), 16-34.

Of Participation in the Life of the Trinity

Using the language of trinitarian theology, St Symeon struggles in *Hymn* 52 with the paradox of the transcendent God's self communication:

> The divine and uncreated superessential nature as tran-
> scending the essence of all created things is called su-
> per-essence, yet still has an essence and is personal,
> [though it is] beyond all essence and is conceived as
> completely incomparable with any created person, for it
> is wholly uncircumscribed by nature. How can you call
> what is indescribable a person? Yet what is not a person
> is nothing—and how is it communicable to me?[45]

In that second "how?" lay a question which was greatly to exercise Greek theologians three hundred years later and result in the distinction between God's essence and energies clearly articulated by St Gregory Palamas.[46] Both SS. Gregory and Symeon were, of course, writing out of a tradition already hundreds of years old. Something like Palamas' distinction can be found in St Maximus the Confessor,[47] Dionysius the Areopagite,[48] the Cappadocian fathers,[49] and even earlier, although it is Palamas who gives it

45 *H* 52.21-28 (M, 263).

46 See B. Krivocheine, "Essence créée et essence divine dans la théologie
    spirituelle de S. Syméon le nouveau théologien," in *Messager de
    l'Exarchat du Patriarche Russe en Europe Occidentale* 75/6, 151-170,
    for the most complete examination of this question; and also Julien-
    Fraigneau, 83-84, 159, and 190-191.

47 See, for example, his *Theological Centuries* I.47-50 and .88-90; *PG*
    90.1100B-1101B and 90.1165D-1168C; English, *Philokalia* II, trans.
    by Ware et.al., 123-124 and 160-161. For a discussion on adumbrations
    of the Palamite distinction in Maximus, see L. Thunberg, *Man and the
    Cosmos*, (Crestwood: 1985), 137-143.

48 See the *Divine Names* II.11, V.2, and XI.6; Suchla, 135-136, 181, and
    188; as well as the articles by G. Semmelroth, "Gottes geeinte Vielheit"
    and "Gottes ausstrahlende Licht," in *Scholastik* 25 and 28 (1950 and
    1953): 389-403 and 481-503 respectively.

49 For Basil, see *Ep.* 234.1 (Loeb, St Basil, *The Letters*, v. III, 370-376);
    and for Nyssa, see the texts collected by B. Krivocheine in the latter's

its clearest and final expression.[50] In contrast to his successor, Symeon obviously lacks a "rigorous and consistent terminology, as well as a logical development of his arguments,"[51] just as he is generally uninterested throughout his writings in making "nuanced theological distinctions...as Palamas was forced to do."[52] He was not forced to do so because, first of all, he was not conscious of saying anything new in claiming a share, however paradoxical, in the uncreated glory of the Triune God. No element of controversy marks his writing on this subject, and we may be sure he would have been called on the question had his adversaries thought he was straying into uncharted waters. That which did raise objections were his assertions that this gift is communicated now, that he himself had received it, and that all Christians are called to the same participation.

Secondly, however, the latter is not a minor exception. If for nothing else, Symeon is of great importance for Palamas in just this, his personal and unflagging witness to the Christian vocation of sharing in the light of the world to come. It is difficult not to hear the experience and example of the New Theologian in St Gregory's assertion that "the good things promised to the saints in the world to come...are seen beforehand by these whom the Spirit has made worthy of sanctity."[53] Or again in the statement that

> It is by means of grace that all of God co-indwells with all of those who are worthy, and that the whole of the

"Simplicité de la nature divine et les distinctions en Dieu selon St Grégoire de Nysse," *Messager de l'Exarchat* 23 (1975), 133-170.

50 For a readable summary of this development, see J. Meyendorff, *St Gregory Palamas and Orthodox Spirituality*, trans. by A. Fiske, (Crestwood: 1974), 11-71 and 95-118.

51 Krivochiene, *Light*, 197.

52 Maloney, *Fire and Light*, 213.

53 From *The Hagioritic Tome*; PG 150.1228A, written by St Gregory at the behest of the leaders of Mt. Athos around 1340/41 and bearing their signatures. On this document, see Meyendorff, *St Gregory Palamas*, 95-96.

saints co-inheres wholly with the whole of God. Thus
they receive into themselves God entire and, as a kind
of reward for their struggles in ascending to Him, they
possess Him, Him alone, Who has made them worthy of
becoming His members, and He indwells them as a soul
is entwined with its own body.[54]

That Palamas was not alone in valuing Symeon's witness is borne
out by the number and quality of the manuscripts of the latter's works
which have come down to us from the fourteenth and fifteenth
centuries.[55] Similarly, the renewal of hesychasm in the late eighteenth century is also marked by, among other things, the republish-
ing of the New Theologian in a contemporary Greek translation.[56]
The latter's reprinting again in recent years, together with the
appearance of more modern Greek translations, is certainly connected with the contemporary revival of monasticism on Mt.
Athos.[57] Fifty generations of Orthodox monks have found in
Symeon someone who speaks directly to their most cherished hopes,
to their faith and love for Christ.

Yet, thirdly, it would not be correct to maintain that his
influence was wholly confined to the matter of his personal
witness. While it is true that his language is not consistent, it is
also the case that it inclines far more in the direction of St

---

54 Ibid., 1229A-1232A. The phrase, "wholly within the whole" of God, is
    frequent in Symeon. See, for example, *ED* VI.137-138; *C* 15.72-77
    (deC, 195); and *H* 2.4-9 (M, 17).

55 See Krivocheine, *SC* 96, 63-145 (review of the MSS of the *Catecheses*),
    and the manuscript survey Darrouzès provides in *SC* 122, 38-45.

56 The edition put out by Nicodemus the Hagiorite and Dionysius
    Zagoraios. See Krivocheine, *Light*, 9, for this and the nineteenth-cen-
    tury translation into Russian by Theophan the Recluse.

57 Modern editions include the series *Philokalia ton Neptikon kai As-
    ketikon*, ed. by P. Christou, (Thessalonica: 1983); five volumes of
    Apanta ton Hagion Pateron, (Athens), the first two of which were
    translated by Athonite monks; and most recently, the publication in
    three volumes of the *Sources chrétiennes* text by Orthodox Kypseli,
    (Thessalonica, 1989, 1990, and 1991).

Gregory's clear distinction than away from it. He did have a genuinely "theological" contribution to make. We may approach the question by asking not only "how" it is that the saints see God, but "what" it is which they do see or, better, given that the vision is that light we dwelt on above, what is the nature of the light of glory? Symeon does struggle with this, particularly in a certain oscillation in his writings between talk of a vision of the essence of God or, instead, of the divine energies. He will argue in some passages that we may share in God essentially,[58] or elsewhere that the Mother of God received the Word of God "essentially" in herself[59] and that this union with Him is repeated "essentially (*ousiodos*)" in the saints.[60] In one, unique passage he even states that the sanctified believer "will see...the immaterial essence penetrating in fact the entire soul."[61]

These passages are striking, but it would be a mistake to take Symeon here as advocating the vision of God's essence championed by Latin Scholasticism.[62] The same *Hymn* 50, in fact, where he spoke above of seeing "the immaterial essence" also contains the following:

> God took on wholly the human condition.
> I became wholly God by communion with God
> perceptibly and consciously, not by essence, though,
> but by participation [*metousia*], as one must
> absolutely believe in order to be Orthodox.[63]

Here communion in the essence of God is specifically ruled out and, for good measure, the assertion that one may share in God

58 See *ED* IV.582.

59 *ED* VII.130.

60 See *ED* I.3.82-86; X.885-889; *H* 51.136ff (M, 261), and 52.55-60 (M, 264).

61 *H* 50.238-241 (M, 255).

62 See the article by Lanne, "Interprétation Palamite," 42-44. For the vision of the essence, see also Lossky, *The Vision of God*, 9-21.

63 *H* 50.199-202 (M, 254).

only "by participation" is held up as the measure of Orthodoxy. This statement also accords with the overwhelming majority of Symeon's statements touching on communion with God. We find him repeating the essence/participation (*ousia/metousia*) distinction again in *Hymn* 1, a passage which stresses the paradoxical nature of the experience.[64] Elsewhere he states that

> ...it is not possible for the creature thus
> to know the Creator entire, as He knows Himself
> *by nature*, rather it is *by grace* that all the angels
> and every created nature sees and knows [Him].[65]

In still other passages it is not God's essence which we see but specifically His energies,[66] or His power,[67] or the shining of His glory.[68] On two occasions, Symeon declares that not even the angels look directly on the divine nature or essence, but instead behold its glory.[69] He argues in *Discourse* VII below that, although God is in Christ to heal, illumine, vivify, clothe and indwell us, and although He is truly present in these actions and indeed is the action, He still transcends them all.[70]

In light of these statements it seems best to take Symeon's remarks on "essential" knowledge and communion in God as signifying his insistence, consistent throughout all his works, on what Archbishop Basil calls the "authenticity" of that participation in the divine which the New Theologian holds out to his readers.[71] "Essentially" would therefore mean "truly" or

64 *H* 1.24ff, esp. 28-29 (M, 11); see also *ED* VII.508-535, for the use of *kata methexin*.

65 *H* 2.95-99 (M, 19).

66 H *24.10-11 (M, 126)* and H 21.43-44 (M, 96).

67 *H* 21.149-152 (M, 98); *H* 30.6-7 (M, 160); *H* 53.92ff (M, 269) and 53.95-96 (M, 269); and *H* 29.162-170 (M, 156).

68 *H* 23.230-239 (m, 118); *H* 31.45-52 (M, 174); and *H* 35.46-64 (M, 192).

69 *H* 22.67-68 (M, 108); and *H* 31.22-64 (M, 173-174).

70 *ED* VII.356-383. Christ gives of His light, life, etc. and is called by each of these names

71 Krivocheine, "Essence créée," esp. 166-170.

"really," i.e., that there is a genuine contact, a touching of God, but never an identity or a merger. The union is always inexplicable. The uncreated cannot mingle with the creature, but, incredibly, it has, and the impossible become somehow impossibly possible defeats the capacities of language. It demands the oxymoron:

> ...they shall see invisibly the invisible beauty... They shall hold Him untouchably...comprehend incomprehensibly His imageless image, His formless form, His shape without shape which, in sight without seeing and in beauty uncompounded, is ever varied and unchanging.[72]

The heart of the paradox is the mystery of the Word made flesh Who offers His glory to all Who desire Him. The One of Whom Symeon speaks in the passage just cited is Christ. The Lord Jesus is the object of the vision of glory and the source of the "light which is discovered suddenly within us."[73] In a passage from *Hymn* 11 which unites the themes of light, Trinity, Christ, personal witness and paradox, Symeon writes:

> For it is in the light of the Spirit that they see who see,
> and those who see in the Latter behold the Son,
> and who has been made worthy of seeing the Son sees
>   the Father
> which even now, as I said, has been accomplished in me.
> As in a [single] drop all the waters are revealed...
> So, greeting the whole in a part, I both see
> Him and worship Him, my Christ and my God.[74]

The vision of the mystery is only partial, incomplete. Symeon compares it elsewhere to holding up a lantern at night on the seashore. The viewer

> ...knows well enough what he is looking at is the sea, a fathomless ocean beyond his ability to view completely...

---

72 *ED* IV.856-861, and see Fraigneau-Julien, 109 and 191.

73 *H* 24.19 (M,126).

74 *H* 11.50-54 and 60-65 (M, 37).

> from that small part that he does see, he forms an idea
> of the infinity of the waters.[75]

He knows well enough, most of the time, to avoid calling this a
vision of the divine essence, since the secrecy of God's inner being
remains inviolate. Instead, he looks for other terms—glory, energies, power, might, grace and light—to account for his experience.
All of these, as Symeon knew, had been employed before him in
the tradition he drew upon. At the same time, he insists that the
light he sees and God are not two different things:

> The light of divinity is not one thing and God another.
> Rather, He is Himself One, both the dwelling and the
> One Who dwells in it, in as much indeed as God Himself
> is light.[76]

One may justly argue that he lacks the precision of a Palamas,
but it still appears inarguable to us that Symeon has assembled
all the elements, and in a uniquely powerful way, that would
later go into his successor's synthesis. It was therefore with
some justification that a seventeenth-century Jesuit referred to
him once as *fons omnis erroris Palamici* ("source of all of
Palamas' errors"),[77] and with even more justification that the
Orthodox celebrate him with the title, "New Theologian."

Of the Word Made Flesh

If Symeon made a real contribution to the theology of the Trinity
(even if as yet unexploited) and helped point the way toward
Palamas' distinction, his teaching on the union of God and man
in Christ offers nothing more, nor less, than the witness "of a
perfect Orthodoxy, one which is both conciliar and patristic,"[78]
and backed by the force of his experience. St Athanasius' phrase,

---

75 *Theological Discourse* II, 263-273 (*McG*, 132).

76 *C* 33.164-166 (*deC*, 343).

77 Cited by Holl, 3.

78 Krivocheine, *Light*, 308-309.

"God became man that we may be made God (*hina hemeis theopoiethomen*),"[79] remained the leitmotif of Christology in the Eastern Christian world, both Greek and Syrian,[80] throughout the long years of debate which troubled the Church from the fourth through the eighth centuries. It was the basis of the great conciliar decisions of Nicea (325 A.D.) and Constantinople (381), of Ephesus (431), Chalcedon (451), Constantinople II (553), III (681), and Nicea II (787). The first two affirmed that the One Who took flesh from Mary was true God, "of one essence with the Father," while the third followed Cyril of Alexandria against Nestorius by declaring that the Second Person of the Trinity and Mary's Son, Jesus, are one and the same. Chalcedon argued against Eutychius that the Lord, though one in Person (*hypostasis*), was as complete in His human nature (*physis*) as in His divinity. Constantinople II, led by the Emperor Justinian, returned to the theme of Ephesus by expressly identifying the *hypostasis* of Chalcedon with the Person of the Word. Christ's humanity is "enhypostatized (*enhypostaton*)" in His Person, such that the answer to the question, "Who is the man Jesus?" becomes unambiguously "God the Word enfleshed."[81] Thus the Christology of the Church, in Father Georges Florovsky's phrase, is "asymmetric." Christ is double in nature, divine and human, but His Person is unique, the *hypostasis* of the Word. The third council of Constantinople,

---

79 *de Inc.* 54.3, *SC* 199, 458; and *Adv.Haer*. V, Preface, *SC* 153, 14, ANF
    I, 526.

80 See S. Brock on St Ephrem, *Hymns on Paradise* (Crestwood, 1990),
    72-74.

81 Secondary studies of this debate are innumerable, but see esp. A.
    Grillmeier, *Christ in Christian Tradition* II,1, (1982), 3-19; J. Meyen-
    dorff, *Christ in Eastern Christian Thought* (Washington, D.C., 1969);
    J. Pelikan, *Emergence*, 226-277, and *The Mind of Eastern Christendom*
    (Chicago, 1974), 37-90; and, specifically on Justinian and the fifth
    Ecumenical Councils, the introduction and texts translated by P. Wes-
    che, *On the Person of Christ: The Christology of the Emperor Justinian*
    (Crestwood, 1991).

inspired by the teaching and example of SS. Maximus the Confessor and Pope Martin I, balanced the equation again by reaffirming Chalcedon: the Lord Jesus' humanity is complete, possessed of its own will (*thelema*) and activity (*energeia*), and a place is thereby secured for the meaning of our human appropriation of the sanctification accomplished and offered us by the incarnate Word.[82]

The seventh and last of the great imperial councils, Nicea II, crowns the long debate by drawing certain conclusions from its predecessors *via* its replies to the objections raised by the Iconoclast movement to the Church's longstanding veneration of images. Taking up the summary of Orthodox theology and especially Christology put together by St John of Damascus, and looking to the consequences which the latter drew from these and applied to the question of icons,[83] the council affirmed that the Incarnation, death, and resurrection of Christ have affected all of creation.[84] Because of Christ, the very physical and material world has become capable of divinity, and the risen humanity of Jesus is the beginning of a new and divinized creation, the Church, whose presence at work in the world here below is signaled by the saints whose images, in turn, adorn the Church building—together with those of Christ and the Theotokos—and receive the veneration due them.[85]

82 See G. Florovsky, *The Byzantine Fathers of the 6th to 8th Centuries*, (Belmont, Massachusetts, 1987), esp. 54-55 for "asymmetry" and 228-246 for Maximus' christology and anthropology.

83 See the *Exp.fid*. 150-181 and 83 (Kotter II, 119-177 and 106-108; English in *NPNF* IX, 2d series, 45-76 and 88); for John on the images, see Kotter III, esp. 75-78, 80-83, 89-92, 105-110, 132-135; English, *St John of Damascus on the Holy Images*, trans. by D. Anderson (Crestwood, 1980), esp. 15-16, 8, 23-25, 26-30, 58-59, 61-62, 72-73, and 80-82.

84 See the decrees of the Council, in English, in *NPNF* XIV, 2d series, 548-555, and for a readable analysis, J. Pelikan *Imago Dei* (Princeton, 1990), esp. 67-119.

85 Pelikan, *Imago*, 121-151.

Throughout this long development we find a constant faithfulness to, and working out of, the implications of deification. That God became man in Jesus of Nazareth means not only the redemption from sin and death, but the partaking of His very divinity. The "paternal light" shining from His deified flesh, to use St Irenaeus' language, becomes the Christian's birthright in Baptism, an inheritance which is to be "realized" through the latter's conscious appropriation, *via* the ascetic ordeal, of the divine energies which inform the virtues.[86] That light, moreover, the splendor of divinity, pervades the whole life of the Church, in particular her sacraments and worship generally, since she is the presence in this world of the world to come. The Church is the "body of Christ," the continuation of the Incarnation, the unique "sacrament" or "mystery" of the new creation. She is the "divine man," and reflected as such in each of the faithful.[87]

This is St Symeon's inheritance from the fathers and the great councils, and all of it is reflected in his own thought and writings. We have already touched on much of it: the ascetic struggle as personal appropriation of the presence of Christ, the light of Christ, and the sacraments as imparting Him. We shall turn below to Symeon's understanding of the human being and will conclude by returning to his vision of the Church which we sketched above in our summary of *Discourse* I. For now, we shall note the echo of the Christological controversies and their resolution in his works. A few examples should suffice to indicate the whole, particularly since we have dwelt above on the central place Christ holds in the New Theologian's piety and experience.

86 See again Florovsky's summary of Maximus in *Byzantine Fathers*, 228-246, and, for the importance of the "ordeal" from New Testament texts through the fathers, his *Ascetics and Spiritual Fathers* (Belmont, Massachusetts, 1987), esp. 17-59.

87 See our discussion below, pp. 147-156, "Of the Image of God in Man."

In the following passage from *Discourse* I we hear the language of the first five councils. Gabriel greets the Mother of God and

> ...together with the word of greeting, the personal (*enhypostatos*), co-essential (*homoousios*), and co-eternal Word of the Father entered wholly into the womb of the maid, and, by the descent and co-operation (*synergia*) of His co-essential Spirit, took on flesh endowed with intelligence and soul (*sarka ennoun kai empsychomenen*) from her all-pure blood, and became man...thus occurred the exchange of God with men. He was united without confusion [*asygchytos*—one of the terms of Chalcedon] with our corruptible and wretched nature and essence Who is Himself beyond nature and super-essential. For the Virgin gave birth from two natures (*physeis*)—I mean the divinity and humanity—to one Son, perfect God and perfect man...[88]

The Lord's solidarity with humanity by virtue of His own human nature, united to Him then and forever, creates the possibility for human participation in His divinity. We become, at least in potential, "gods by grace," and

> ...one, I say, [with God] not in our persons, but one in the nature of divinity and humanity. We are one in the nature of divinity in becoming ourselves gods by adoption [*thesei*]...On the other hand we are one in the nature of humanity as His kinfolk, and as having been accorded the name of His brothers...

The agent of our entry into the union between God and man effected by Christ, Symeon continues in this passage, is the same Holy Spirit Who overshadowed the Virgin at the annunciation.

> For God, Who is Spirit...wills that by the Holy Spirit we be united to Him, cleave to Him, become one body and co-heirs with Him.[89]

---

88   *ED* I.9.57-68.

89   *ED* II.7.193-207.

"What," he asks in his *Theological Chapters*, is "the purpose of the Word of God's economy" if it is not in order that, "having partaken of what is ours, He might make us communicants of what is His own" and "lead our race up by grace to what is His by nature?"[90] Once "having become God by adoption, I see Him Who is God by nature."[91] Reflecting the accents of Chalcedon and subsequent councils, together with St Athanasius' language of theosis, he states that God, by taking flesh, "has deified me altogether whom He has assumed."[92] As a result, God who became "double" has made those who receive Him "double" in return: "He took my flesh and gave me Spirit...as man I possess nothing of what is exalted, but now...I possess Christ the Lord."[93] This "exchange" entails a real communication between the natures of God and man: "For when He took a body, He gave His Holy Spirit, and is united essentially through the latter to all the faithful, and this union is inseparable."[94] He, Symeon, remains what he is by nature yet is endowed with another mode of being which is divine, uncreated. In a singular passage from *Hymn 25* he experiences the paradox. Christ appears to him as light while he is sitting at night in the darkness of his cell, "and I became light in the night while in the midst of darkness." He sees both the light and darkness at once. Neither one vanishes, nor is one mingled with the other: "O dreadful wonder! I look in double form with doubled pairs of eyes, [the one] of the soul and [the other] of the body."[95]

The eyes of the soul are opened only by the works of faith. Otherwise, Symeon argues, there would be no difference between believers and unbelievers. Those who crucified the Lord would have to be reckoned as seeing the Father if there were

---

90 *Ch* III.88; *SC* 51, 108-109 (McG, 99).
91 *H* 52.52-53 (M, 264).
92 Ibid. 47-51.
93 *H* 25.64-78 (M, 136-137).
94 *H* 51.140-142 [AK, 139-141], (M, 26); and see also H 7.26-24 (M, 28-29).
95 *H* 25.42-61 (M, 136).

no distinction between fleshly vision and the "revelation of
divinity."[96] The second Person of the Trinity "emptied himself" to share in our clay, and we are obliged in turn to imitate
His self-emptying to share in His glory.[97] For Symeon the
Incarnation did not stop with Christ's birth, but included His
passion and death.[98] Here is the role allotted the human will
and, with it, the echoes of the sixth ecumenical council and
Maximus the Confessor.[99] Christ is the unique goal of humanity for Whom and by Whom all were made. In His saving
economy He has renewed human nature, has accomplished all
that was necessary.[100] Yet, the redemption of human freedom
calls for the exercise of that freedom, for willed conformity
with Christ's acts of grace, "the works of faith" in short.
"Therefore," Symeon has Christ say in *Hymn* 40 "those who
imitate My sufferings shall become co-partakers of My divinity, and shall be co-heirs of My kingdom."[101] The conciliar
definitions insisted that in Christ human nature has been saved
once and for all, but the same councils and the debates that
shaped their resolutions also insisted on the equal primacy of
"person" and "act" (*energeia*).[102] If our nature has been saved
by the Person of the Word uniting with it and filling it with His
energies, with the common life of the Trinity, it remains for
each human person to will the acceptance of what he or she, in
Christ, already is, and to bring to fruition in deeds the seed

96 *ED* IV.95-105.
97 *C* 27.312-330 (deC, 292-293), from the argument of St Paul in *Phil.* 2.
98 See Völker on Symeon, *Praxis*, 415-416.
99 See our note 82, page 142, and note 86, page 143 above. This is as well
    the burden of Lars Thunberg's magisterial study of Maximus, *Micro-
    cosm and Mediator: The Theological Anthropology of Maximus the
    Confessor* (Lund, 1965).
100 See *C* 19.107-131 (deC, 229); 20.21-43 (deC, 231-232); 28.301-34
    (deC, 303-304); and *H* 40.70-78 (M, 206-207).
101 *H* 40.79-81 (M, 207).
102 See Meyendorff, *Byzantine Theology*, 164 and 182-188, as well as his
    A Study of Gregory Palamas, 180-184.

which Christ, Who is "enpersoned love (*enhypostatos agape*),"[103] has already sown in the hearts of all, and in whose growth He aids the meanwhile unseen.[104]

For St Symeon, as for his predecessors, the human being is created in the image and likeness of God as person and as willing agent. Thus Christ as the redemption and restoration of the image brings us to our author's vision of man fallen and made anew. Here again we shall find at work the familiar combination of fidelity to the tradition and personal witness.

Of the Image of God in Man: Fall and Restoration

The New Theologian assumes an anthropology inherited from the Greek fathers. According to this tradition, the divine economy accomplished in Jesus Christ represents not just the restoration of human nature, but its fulfillment. Christ is that for which humanity was created in the beginning. As St Maximus puts it in his *Ambigua*, "Always and in all things God the Word of God wills to effect the sacrament of His embodiment."[105] While the Confessor was, in the seventh century, perhaps the first to state this truth so clearly, there can be no doubt that it was embedded in the fathers who were his sources. SS. Irenaeus and Gregory of Nyssa, to name but two, advocate very similar views.[106] The fathers' understanding of human nature is essentially dynamic. The human being is created with a capacity for the reception of God, and that in such a way that this capacity

103 See *C* 36.271 (deC, 376).

104 *Ch* III.76-77; *SC* 51, 104 (McG, 94-95).

105 Ambigua VII; *PG* 91.1048D.

106 It seems implied in *Adv.Haer.* III.xvi.6; III.xxii.3; IV.xx.1-7; and IV.xxxviii.1-4 (*SC* 211, 312-314; 438, and *SC* 100, pt. 2, 624-648 and 942-460; and *ANF* I, 442-443; 455; 487-490; and 521-523). For Nyssa, see Christ as the joining and summation of creation, *Great Catechism* 32 (Srawley [Cambridge, 1956], 114-122; and English, *Later Fathers*, 310-312) as well as *de hom. opf.* 16 (*PG* 44.185Bff), 17 (44.188A-192A), and 22 (44.204Bff).

is no mere adjunct or superstructure, a kind of *addendum* or bonus, but in a sense definitive of human nature itself. Put another way, according to this view unless the human person is in communion with God, that person is less than fully human. Human nature presupposes grace. Without grace it becomes unnatural, sub-human. Conceived of as openness to God by its very essence, human life in consequence means motion, a growth into the appropriation of the infinite God which, because God is infinite, can therefore never end.[107]

This is exactly what we find in Symeon. As one of his modern commentators remarks, "It would be completely futile to try to find a single word in his writings where he says anything about 'natural man.' The latter [man] always stands in an inseparable relation to God...either in the positive sense of grace, or in the negative sense of sin."[108] This statement echoes what Symeon himself, speaking in the person of God, says in *Hymn* 53: "That it was altogether for this purpose...that I created Adam: that he should see Me,"[109] as well as elsewhere in his writings.[110] Man was created "double," i.e., as body and created spirit, in order for his "spiritual senses" to be filled with the light of the "sun" of heaven as the physical eye receives the light of the sun which shines on earth.[111] All the faculties of the soul are made to share and become one in the unified perception of the Triune God.[112] Nor is this participation in God limited to the soul. Symeon is no platonist. As we saw above in his use of nuptial imagery for

107 See Irenaeus, *Adv. Haer.* IV.xxxviii.3-4 (*SC* 100, pt.2, 952-960, and *ANF* I, 521-522); and Nyssa, *Great Cat.* 21 (Srawley, 81-84, and *Later Fathers*, 297-298), and *Life of Moses* 18 (*SC* 1, 102-110). For comment on the latter, see Daniélou, *From Glory to Glory*, trans. by Musurillo (Crestwood, 1979), 58-71.

108 Biedermann, *Menschenbild*, 23.

109 *H* 53.205-208 (M, 271).

110 See *C* 6.140-161 (deC, 123), and *C* 19.107-131 (deC, 229).

111 *H* 23.448-475 (M, 123).

112 Thus see *ED* IV.369-514 on the "body" of the virtues.

the union with God, particularly in *Hymn* 15, the entire human body is called to share in the immaterial fire of divinity.[113]

It is the soul, however, which is the primary locus of encounter, and which mediates the energies of the Spirit to the body.[114] Or, put differently, the soul is the place of the image. We are "called to see God only because God is already present in us in a particular way by reason of our kinship with the Word, the perfect image."[115] Like many of his predecessors in the tradition, Symeon understands this likeness or "kinship" to lie in the human capacity for freedom (*autoexousion*).[116] Endowed by the Creator with the potential for growth into virtue and communion, the first couple were called to

> ...follow His commandment and do it with joy. Thus they would be accounted as having acquired the virtues by their own efforts, in order to offer them up as their gift to the Master and so be led up by them progressively to the perfect image and likeness of God, and approach the Unapproachable without suffering bodily death or the danger of being consumed by His fire.[117]

Adam and Eve were not made to know death. The path intended for them was rather voluntary submission to the divine will, an ever increasing appropriation of the God's likeness, a perpetual increase in sharing the uncreated glory.[118] This is the natural "vector" of human existence for Symeon. Indeed, human nature, as he understands it, is this inherent "thrust" or "motion" toward

113 See also *H* 28.150-162 (M, 151-152), and *C* 13.56-89 (deC, 182-183).

114 For example, see *C* 25.85-122 (deC, 269-270) and, on the "heaviness" of the body as a consequence of the Fall, Ibid. 156-199 (deC, 271-272).

115 Julien-Fraigneau, 157.

116 See the study on Gregory of Nyssa in this connection by S. Gaith, *La conception de la liberté chez Grégoire de Nysse* (Paris, 1953), esp. 40-86, and, on Maximus, Polycarp Sherwood's *The Earlier Ambigua of St Maximus the Confessor and his Refutation of Origenism* (Rome, 1955).

117 *ED* X.41-47.

118 See Völker, *Praxis*, 238, citing *C* 17.28ff; and note as well *ED* I.1.50-66, on what might have been without the Fall.

God, and this in turn identifies our nature as fully human only when it is penetrated wholly, body and soul, by the glory of the Resurrection. [119] Yet "nature" is always an abstraction, a potential, unless and until it is realized in action through the assent of a willing subject. Again we return here to Symeon's emphasis, characteristic of the whole Greek tradition, on *hypostasis* and *energeia*, person and act. Adam was created with the potential for kinship or likeness to God. He was called, in a sense, to choose himself, to make his own that vector which comprised his own deepest reality and, in the choosing, discover the presence of, and enter into communion with, his Creator.

The first couple failed. Following a long established tradition, Symeon identifies evil not as a nature, but as the product of choice, an inclination or turning of the willing subject toward that which is not. [120] The result of this turning or perversion of the will in Adam and Eve was catastrophe:

> ...they not only fell away from the greater hope...from entering into the light itself...but were changed as well into corruption and death. They fell into lightless darkness and, becoming slaves to the prince of the dark and ruled over by him, they entered into sin through the darkness of death. [121]

This occurred, he emphasizes, not by force, but by the free will (*thelemati*) both of the first pair and of all who have since come out of them. [122] Echoing Romans 8, Symeon speaks in chapters two, four and five of *Discourse* I of the cosmic effects of the Fall. The world is subjected unwillingly to the corruption of the man for whom it had been created. The results of the first sin are a complete breakdown, literally a stripping off of the glory,

119 See *C* 13.58-89 (deC, 182-183).
120 See *C* 4.63-125 (deC, 71-73) and 5.770-819 (deC, 110-111).
121 *ED* X.50-55. See the whole passage, 36-80, for an illustration of the points above, together with *C* 14.11-36 (deC, 193-194).
122 Ibid.

the "vesture of light," for which humanity was made and a consequent disintegration of the human composite, a "return" to the nothing from which Adam was originally taken:

> ...of dust, corruptible, mortal, deaf, blind, naked and insensible, differing in no way from the irrational animals or, better, become even worse than the beasts... [123]

Even, Symeon adds, if one were somehow to avoid personal sin and refuse to join the idolatry which made gods not only of the natural elements but even of the very passions themselves (he was doubtless thinking of such "gods" as Eros and Aphrodite—but his point would seem to apply to modern equivalents as well, e.g., sexual passion, "creativity," ambition, etc.), still such a person, "since he, too, because of his descent from the seed of those had sinned," would be "a slave to the tyrant, death," and would therefore "also be given over to corruption and sent...to hell." [124] Sin, and particularly death, he sees as the consequences of the Fall, the content of what Western Christian tradition identifies as original sin, and here, too, he stands in continuity with the mainstream of the Greek fathers. [125]

This is the condition from which humanity is rescued in Christ. In Him soul and body are united to the Creator Word and the formerly indwelling curse of death is lifted. The intended composition of human nature as body, soul, and uncreated grace is restored and fulfilled. As Symeon writes in *Discourse* VI below

> ...as the soul is unable to live without being illumined by the Creator, neither does the body live without being empowered by the soul. Attend to the precise meaning of these words: body, soul, and God, these three. God without beginning, without end, unapproachable, unsearchable, invisible, ineffable, intangible...has ap-

123 *ED* XIII.90-96.
124 Ibid.
125 See our note 189, page 119 above.

peared to us in these latter days in the flesh through His Son, has...been made known to us through His all-Holy Spirit as like us in every way save sin, has mingled Himself with a rational soul... for the sake of my soul in order to save my spirit and make my flesh immortal...[126]

Thus, he continues a little later,

...does man, without confusion or division [an echo of Chalcedon] become in God a god by grace in both his soul and body...He Who has paradoxically bound all these together, Who has mingled what is both intelligible and immaterial with clay, unites Himself unconfusedly with both of these, and I myself am in His image and likeness...Body, soul, and God are the man who is created according to the image of God and made worthy of becoming God.[127]

Christ re-establishes the image and likeness once and for all. The obstacles put in humanity's way by an alien tyranny, the rule of the "prince of the dark," are lifted and removed altogether. As the "new Adam," Christ has accomplished everything that the first man was called—and failed—to do.[128] The way is open again for everyone to be clothed anew with the "robe of glory,"

...the original vesture, the very mantle which the Lord wore before the foundation of the world...the Holy Spirit who alters... [us] in a manner appropriate to God, an alteration which is strange, ineffable, and divine...[129]

This is the *theosis* or divinization which we stressed above as the ground of Eastern Christian Christology and soteriology. Its foundation is the Incarnation of the Word which undoes and reverses the results of the Fall.[130] Yet, as we also saw above in

126 *ED* VI.135-145.
127 Ibid. 163-178, and see also IX.19-103, together with *C* 13.56-89 (deC, 182-183).
128 See *ED* I.3 and II.7.
129 *ED* IV.589-594. On the "robe of glory," see our note 83, page 96 above.
130 See Krivocheine, *Light*, 389-390.

our discussion of the virtues, of Baptism, and of the Incarnation itself, the grace offered demands a personal and willed response from its recipients. It remains for all of us, according to Symeon, "to choose ourselves" as we have been recreated in Christ. If He "emptied Himself" to share our clay, we are therefore obliged to share voluntarily in His "shameful death," His cross.[131] The appropriation of redemption, the way of theosis, leads inevitably through the repentance God wanted from Adam and did not receive.[132] It requires the renunciation of one's own, fallen will,[133] the putting aside of the passions,[134] compunction and mourning,[135] and the acquisition of the virtues. All this is simply in order that one may become fully natural again, since to fulfill God's commandments is to be engaged in the proper work allotted to Adam.[136] Life on this earth is therefore given to the Christian for ascesis. It is the time when, in Christ and in conformity to His passion, the believer may discover his or her true self.[137] At every stage the grace of the Holy Spirit is present and active. This grace is imperceptible at first but, as the appropriation of salvation proceeds and "by virtue of the likeness produced by nature and grace, man the image of God becomes capable of knowing the Original in himself:"

> I see Him within...
> suddenly become manifest,
> both united inexpressibly
> and ineffably joined
> and mingled with me unmingledly
> like fire with iron itself

131 *C* 27.268-299 (deC 292-292) and *C* 6.300-340 (deC, 127-128).
132 See *C* 5.160-252 (deC, 94-96).
133 See *C* 34.214-243 (deC, 353-354), and *C* 6.282-299 (deC, 127).
134 See, for example, *C* 9.303-367 (deC, 158-160).
135 For example, *C* 14.24-27 (deC, 187-189).
136 See *C* 10.100-103 (deC, 164).
137 See *C* 17.12-61 (deC, 204-206).

and light within a crystal,
and He has made me like fire
...like light.[138]

The image of light shining through crystal is singularly apt. The struggle of ascesis is "suddenly" revealed as the way of *theosis* because in Christ the deification of human nature has already been accomplished, the image has been restored and the creature "mingled unmingledly" with the Creator. Human ascetic effort is therefore a kind of "polishing" of the crystal, a wiping away of clinging dust—the dust of attachment to trifles, trivialities and worthless dross (Symeon uses much stronger language for the appurtenances of mortal life which draw people away from God[139])—in order to discover beneath it the presence of the One in Whom humanity has already fulfilled its vocation and become the habitation of divinity. Like trying to read by a light bulb covered with grime, we cannot see the Light Who abides within us unless and until we have bent the elbow and polished the glass of our soul.

This, Symeon maintains in *Discourse* I, is just what the saints have done. As a result,

...the souls of the saints adhere to God while still in the body, by grace of the Holy Spirit and of their union with Him.[140]

They see God. They acquire His "mind" and understanding.[141] They are already citizens of the kingdom and temples of the Trinity,[142] dwell in the light of the world to come,[143] and have

138 *H* 30.421-430 (M, 168).
139 What are silks, he asks in one place, but the "excrement of worms" (*ED* VI.230-231)? Elsewhere, in *ED* IV.314-339, he declares that the things of this world are scrap and carrion, and goes on to compare the people preoccupied with them to dogs barking and tearing at butcher's offal.
140 *ED* I.5.109-111.
141 *H* 39.61-66 (M, 203).
142 *Ch* I.79 (*SC* 51, 64; McG, 56).
143 *ED* X.132-136.

become themselves treasuries of the knowledge of the scriptures, "bearing in themselves both new and old mysteries inscribed in them by the finger of God."[144] They are already in heaven, and their growth in the glory given once for all in Christ will increase following their physical deaths:

> ...after falling asleep [their souls] are renewed and changed, and raised from death, and established again in great glory, in the light without evening.[145]

The final stage of the saints' appropriation of the image restored in Christ awaits the resurrection on the last day when their bodies, "too, shall be made incorruptible...when...the whole earthly creation...will be changed and united with the heavenly."[146] Then "their perfection will be ever incomplete, and [their] advance into glory shall continue without end."[147]

What, though, of those who have not cleansed the lens of their conscience and will? They, Symeon replies, have willfully turned away from their own renewal. In effect, they have refused themselves. Even God, in *Hymn* 34, confesses His inability to save them:

> What then should I do with them? I am altogether at a loss.
> For to save them by compulsion in spite of themselves,
> This would also seem a tribulation to them, since they refuse to be saved.[148]

The image is always honored, and God Himself will not bruise the freedom of even the damned. The latter are at war with themselves. The image renewed in Christ is their own deepest truth, but, if they have not recognized this in life, then they will continue to be blind in the world to come. The same light which is heaven for the just

---

144 *Ch* III.100 (*SC* 51, 112-113; McG, 102-103).

145 *ED* I.5.112-114.

146 Ibid. 115-119.

147 *H* 1.213-214 (M, 16).

148 *H* 34.115-117 (M, 190).

will therefore be the fire of hell for the damned. Their interior
warfare becomes palpable and inescapable:

> ...the sinners shall be in the midst of it [the light]
>   enclosed in darkness,
>
> not seeing, nor having any divine perception at all,
>
> but burning up in their conscience
>
> and by it condemned. Their sorrow and
>   their pain will be unutterable and everlasting.[149]

For Adam's sake the creation was submitted to corruption.
In the new Adam the universe is restored, and Symeon is also
very much the theologian

Of the New Creation: the Church and the World to Come

One recent critic writes that the New Theologian "can
certainly be criticized in that he stressed the individual and
subjective element of Christian life one-sidedly" while seem-
ing "to forget the objective structure of the Church."[150] Archbishop Basil's view is a more balanced one. The saint's
"profound faith in the Church as the body of Christ...goes
hand in hand with a rather dim view of the condition in which
the Church found itself in his day."[151] The key would seem to
lie in the phrase "objective structure." We have seen that
Symeon's emphasis lies unquestionably on the charismatic
and "subjective" (for want of a better word) side of Christian
life, but this is a long way from saying that he dismisses its
institutional and "objective" aspect. His fierce criticism of the
clergy of his day must be weighed against his equally angry
descriptions of his fellow monks, and against his heartfelt
reverence for the priestly office as well. He may have sat
lightly to the *magisterium* of the hierarchy of his day, particularly if that ran contrary to his own conviction and experience,

149 *H* 1.227-231 (M, 16); see also *ED* X.11ff and esp. 82ff.
150 Van Rossum, "Priesthood," 224.
151 Krivocheine, *Light*, 327-328.

but he held as a certainty that the decrees of the Ecumenical Councils were inspired. He did denounce a mechanical view of the sacraments which held that the latter save by conveying the presence of the Spirit without the Latter being consciously perceived, but the role which Baptism and especially the Eucharist play in his thought, devotion, and experience is never less than central. The "objectively" constituted Church, both as eschatological reality and as historically existing in the institutional forms which it had received from the Apostles, is never far from the New Theologian's mind and heart. There is no indication in his works that he ever dreamed of contesting it. He certainly never forgot it.

For Symeon the Church is reality with a capital "R." It is *more* real or objective a truth than the phenomenal world, the universe embraced by the five senses and the Fall. Like the Neoplatonism of late antiquity, which came to him via Church fathers such as Gregory of Nyssa, Dionysius the Areopagite, and Maximus the Confessor, he holds that the unseen, intelligible world is the more truly existing one.[152] Unlike the pagan philosophers, however, and together with the fathers, his view here is firmly rooted in the New Testament. The Resurrection of Christ has ushered in a new condition of existence, a new and different mode of being. His risen body, animated by the Holy Spirit, becomes the first fruits of the new creation, "for in Him dwells the whole fullness of the divinity bodily" (Col 2:9) and "from this fullness have we all received" (John 1:16)—phrases, for example, that Symeon quotes in the concluding chapters of Discourse II. In the latter work he traces God's saving economy in terms of the "portion" God took from Adam to fashion Eve. The history of salvation is the story of this "portion" from Eve through Noah and Abraham to David and finally to the Virgin Mother:

152 See Biedermann, *Menschenbild*, 117.

> God took from the Virgin flesh endowed with a mind
> and soul... Having taken this same from her, He gave it
> His own Spirit, the Holy Spirit, and enlarged it with
> what it had not had before: life everlasting...in order for
> Him to re-create the nature of Adam...so that the chil-
> dren who would be born of God might receive regenera-
> tion through the Holy Spirit, and then that all who
> believe in Him might become, in the Spirit, God's own
> kin and so comprise [with Him] one single body.[153]

Because Christ has become "our kinsman" in the flesh, He has
also made "us co-participants in His divinity" and, since the
latter

> cannot be broken down in parts...all of us who partake
> of it in truth must necessarily be one body with Christ
> in the one Spirit.[154]

The flesh of Christ establishes His abiding link with humanity. It is Adam's own flesh, taken from him to form the woman,
Eve. But with the new Eve, Mary, this flesh is filled with the
glory of the Word: "For Your spotless and divine body flashes
wholly with the fire of Your divinity, [with which it] is entwined
and mingled ineffably."[155] This is what is imparted to the
Christian in Baptism and Eucharist via the medium of the Spirit.
Hence the three ways by which Symeon says the saints are
kinsmen of the Mother of God. Thus he can state that "[we]
confess and believe that by partaking of the Lord's deified flesh
which came from her we partake of everlasting life."[156] We can
share in His flesh because, "when He had risen incorruptible
from the dead, He also raised up His body as wholly divine,
spiritual and immaterial,"[157] and that divinity, therefore, which
now quickens His risen flesh is imparted to the believers:

153 *ED* II.7.144-169.
154 *ED* I.6.80-82.
155 *H* 2.7-9 (M, 17).
156 *ED* I.10.171-173.
157 *ED* I.3.60-62.

> When we receive the Spirit of our Master and God, we
> become participants of His divinity and essence, and
> when we eat of His all-pure flesh—I mean in the [sac-
> rament of] holy communion—we become truly His kin,
> of one body with Him. [158]

This, he exclaims, is

> ...the beginning of a new portion and a new world...Up to
> this point all were shadows and types...But this, this is the
> truth. This is both the renovation and renewal of the whole
> world...He Who is Son God does...not beget children in a
> fleshly way, but He re-fashions us instead spiritually. [159]

At present this mystery remains hidden, but it continues to
happen "even to the present day" in the bodies of the saints,
and Symeon points to the incorruption of the latters' relics as
proof. [160] The full manifestation awaits the general resurrection
and the world to come, when "the whole earthly creation, this
visible and perceptible world, will be changed and united with
the heavenly." [161]

Heaven, in a sense, is already a fact, already here. "It seems
to me," Symeon says, "that the fully ripened world is the Church
of Christ." [162] Quoting 2 Cor 11:2, Ps 45:13-15, John 3:16, and
alluding at the same time to Rev 21:21 and Eph 2:13-22, he
gathers together the New Testament images of the Church as the
"bride of Christ," the "one new man," the new Jerusalem, in
order to conclude that these texts "demonstrate that the temple
of God the King, His city and world, is the Church." [163] As the
world to come, the Church is still in process of completion. Not
in the sense that anything more is needed for her establishment,

158 Ibid. 83-86.
159 *ED* II.7.1-5 and 27-30.
160 *ED* I.3.79-83.
161 *ED* I.5.116-119.
162 *ED* I.7.3-4.
163 Ibid. 44-45.

since that was accomplished in Christ. Rather, according to the eternal providence of God—and here he cites Eph 4:13, Heb 12:23, and particularly Rev 8:29-30—all

> those who are foreknown by God must be born, come into being, before the world beyond our world, the world of the Church...of the heavenly Jerusalem, is filled up.[164]

So far as our experience applies, limited as it is by the constraints on our perceptions which are themselves bound by space and time, the Church is still a-building, but in the counsels of God it is present. This presence is made known in the experience of the saints and is available to all in the Eucharist.

We have seen above how Symeon emphasizes the personal encounter with God incarnate, whether in terms of the vision of glory, the conscious perception of the Presence in the sacraments, the conversation of the soul alone with God Alone, or for that matter, in his related and stubborn resistance to the hierarchy's demands that he conform to ecclesiastical "due process" in his veneration of the elder who had led him to Christ. His personal emphasis also comes out in his discussion of the Church in *Discourse* I. The "marriage" of God and the Church is realized in each of the saints. Mary the Theotokos is the original and paradigm of this marriage, but "for each one of the faithful and sons of light this same marriage is performed in like and scarcely diverging manner."[165] Symeon explains how this happens in chapter ten of *Discourse* I. He is first of all careful to underline that the Virgin's marriage is unique,

> since it was once and for all that the Word of God became flesh [from her]...and was born, bodily...and since it is not possible that He should take flesh once more.[166]

164 *ED* I.8.11-14.
165 *ED* I.9.76-78.
166 *ED* I.10.51-55.

The, as it were, objective conditions of personal communion with the Word are established once and once only, hence the altogether irreplaceable and exalted role of the Virgin. Hence, too, that Reality of the Church which is more true and more real than the visible world, and which is communicated to the believer in the sacraments. Symeon's reference in the following is to the Eucharist:

> ...the same undefiled flesh which He accepted from the pure loins of Mary...and with which He was given birth in the body, He gives to us as food. And when we eat of it...each one of us receives within himself the entirety of God made flesh, our Lord Jesus Christ...present in the body bodilessly, mingled with our essence and nature, and deifying us who share His body, who are become flesh of His flesh and bone of His bone.[167]

It is this union which he calls "the second mode of birth" of God the Word. It occurs "in the divine Spirit...which is ever working in our hearts the mystery of the renewal of human souls."[168] By communicating in the deified flesh of Christ, the saints are elevated "to the ranks of His mother...His brothers, and...His kinsmen."[169] This, he concludes, "is the mystery of the marriages which the Father arranged for His only-begotten Son."[170]

In the New Theologian's account of the mystical marriage there is clearly an interweaving of what we may call the ecclesial and the mystical, or—perhaps better—a real identity. The Church is truly the "Temple of the King," but so equally is the individual believer the "temple of the Holy Spirit" and "tabernacle" of Christ.[171] The Church is the new world re-cre-

---

167 Ibid. 55-72.
168 Ibid. 92-94.
169 Ibid. 111-114.
170 Ibid. 185-186.
171 See 1 Cor 3:16-17 and . 2 Cor 5:1-5, and, relatedly, *ED* X.350-369 and 426-447, for the notion of Scripture as the "mirror of the soul."

ated in the Word incarnate, the universe of the age to come. But so, Symeon argues in *Discourse* VI, is "each one of us...created by God as second world, a great world in this small and visible one," and all are commanded to possess "the sun or righteousness shining within us" and "to provide our neighbor with the example of the immaterial day, the new earth and new heaven."[172] This parallelism or identity runs throughout his thought. In *Discourse* III, for example, he assumes a parallel between the individual Christian as throne of God and the seraphim of Isaiah's vision who bear aloft the God of Israel[173] while, in his *Hymns*, he stands in awe before the throne of God when serving as priest "of the divine mysteries" at the altar,[174] and trembles before the same mystery revealed in his heart.[175] The Church which is Christ's body is paralleled by the "body of virtues" which is the mature man in Christ.[176] The Church is the world to come in *Discourse* I and, in *Discourse* X, the Day of the Lord shines in the hearts of the saints while still in this life.[177] Again in *Discourse* X, the two poles of ecclesial and mystical mirror one another and are specifically tied together in the Eucharist:

> His holy flesh is not flesh alone, but flesh and God insepa-
> rably yet without confusion: visible in the flesh, i.e., in the
> bread for physical eyes while invisible in its divinity for
> those same eyes, yet seen by the eyes of the soul.[178]

Church and believer, altar and heart, confirm and reflect one another, and both turn around and partake of the one mystery,

172 *ED* VI.794-801 and 826-834. See *SC* 129, 64, note a. for references to Symeon's sources here in Gregory of Nazianzus. See also John Damascene, *Ex.fid.* 26 (Kotter II, 76 and 79).
173 *ED* III.669-698.
174 *H* 19.33-103 (M, 85-87).
175 *H* 8.63-73 (M, 31); 13.32-81 (M, 44-46); and 16.18-30 (M, 58).
176 *ED* IV.697-737.
177 *ED* S.697-737.
178 Ibid. 764-769.

Christ. Each is, as it were, the icon or sacramental image of the other through which the presence of the Word enfleshed is communicated. Without that deifying and vivifying power both are equally idols—mere flesh or naked institution[179]—just as the Eucharist itself is, without the perception of the "eyes of the soul," merely bread,[180] and the Lord Jesus not God but a failed prophet.[181] It is faith which reveals the wandering preacher from Nazareth as true God, the Eucharist as the bread from heaven, and the Church and the believer—the great world and the small—as complementary expressions of the Eighth Day and age to come.

Before turning to St Symeon's definitive discussion of this theme in *Discourse* XIV below, we should briefly note his sources. It is the ancient idea of the microcosmos (man) reflecting the macrocosmos (universe), and it goes back a long way in the tradition of Greek philosophy. Plato uses it in the *Republic*, where the ideal state is portrayed as the rational man writ large, and it is central to thinkers in the Stoic tradition who saw the universe reflected in the individual.[182] Plotinus fuses Plato and the Stoics to produce the doctrine that each person is a *kosmos noetos* (intelligible world).[183] His successors, the later Neoplatonists, carry on a vision of reality which is at once an analysis in detail of the "great chain of being" and a dissection of the human psyche as reflecting at once the structures of the

---

179 Hence Symeon's furious denunciations of the lust for secular or ecclesiastical preferment; see *ED* XI.324ff, on begging God that one not be so honored even if called by Him.

180 See Völker, *Praxis*, 405.

181 *ED* X.738-741.

182 See *Ennead* III.4.3. (Loeb, 148-150). See also Cochrane, *Christianity and Classical Culture* (New York, 1957, rev.), 74-98; W. Jaeger, *Paidea*, v. II, *In Search of the Divine Center* (Oxford, 1986, rep.), 347-357; and A.H. Armstrong, *An Introduction to Ancient Philosophy* (London, 1965), 142-144.

183 Ibid. On the fusion of Stoa and Plato in Plotinus, see Armstrong, *Introduction*, 175-186.

sensory world and the intelligible universe of eternal forms.[184]
While none of these writers is likely to have had a direct
influence on Symeon, he was certainly influenced by their
impress on Church fathers whom he had read.

This is not to say that the Greek fathers were Platonists pure
and simple. The relationship between Christianity and Hellenism
is in any case an issue of vast complexity. Suffice it to say here
that the fathers sought to express the revelation in Christ with the
vocabulary and ways of thought most ready to hand and, by the
third and fourth centuries A.D., that meant in turn Neoplatonic
philosophy. Their struggle over just how to do so without at the
same time betraying the faith comprises the history of Greek
patristic theology from its beginnings in St Justin Martyr to the
consummation of Byzantine thought in St Gregory Palamas. The
New Theologian is part of that continuum.

Specifically with regard to the question of mystical experience and the eschatological nature of the Church, and the meeting
of the two in the Church's sacraments, especially the Eucharist,
the chain of development is a long one. The New Testament
provides us with our starting point. The Church is the "fullness of
Him [Christ] Who fills all in all," the "one new man," the city and
temple of God, the spiritual Sinai, the "body of Christ," the
vine.[185] It is in short the presence of the kingdom of heaven.
Christ's preaching of the kingdom in the Synoptic Gospels identifies the former variously as like a "mustard seed," hidden leaven,
a pearl, a lost coin, and as present "within."[186] In the Gospel of

184 For the phrase and concept "great chain of being," see A. Lovejoy, *The
    Great Chain of Being* (New York, 1960), and for the simultaneity of
    micro- and macrocosm in Neoplatonism, S. Gersh, *From Iamblichus to
    Erieugena*, 27-120.
185 For the "fullness of Him," etc. Eph. 1:23; "one new man," Ibid. 2:15;
    the city and temple, Rev. 21:2-4 and 22-23; Sinai, Heb. 12:22; "body
    of Christ," *R* 12:5; and the "vine" Jn 15:1ff.
186 For the "mustard seed," Mt 13:31-32 and Mk 4:30-32; hidden leaven,
    Mt 13:33; pearl, Mt 13:44-46; "within you," Lk 17:21.

John the kingdom is Christ Himself: "I am," He says at different points, "the Way," "the Truth," "the Life," "the Door," "the Shepherd," "the Resurrection," the "living water," "the Vine," and the true "bread from heaven."[187] Water, vine and bread are further connected with the Church's worship, specifically Baptism and the Eucharist. The disciples thus recognize the risen Jesus in "the breaking of bread" in Luke 24. In Acts 2, the "breaking of bread" and Baptism identify the early Christians as the new community of the Messiah. As the Church unites heaven and earth in Colossians 1:16-20, so does its earthly worship, the earthly liturgy, reflect and partake of the eternal liturgy of the angels in Hebrews 12:22-23 and, especially, Revelation, chapters four and five.[188] All the elements for what we have described so far in Symeon thus appear to be present in the Christian scriptures.

It would be some time, however, before all of those elements would come together. One line, the Church's worship as mirroring the heavenly liturgy, runs through early Jewish-Christian writings, like the *Shepherd of Hermas*, to Clement of Alexandria, Gregory of Nyssa, Theodore of Mopsuestia, and Germanos of Constantinople in the late eighth, early ninth century—to name a few.[189] Another, not at all exclusive of the

187 For the "way, the truth and the life," Jn 14:6; "the door," 10:7; "the shepherd," 10:11; "the Resurrection," 11:25; and "living water," 7:38.

188 On these passages in Rev. see Petersen, *The Angels and the Liturgy*, trans. by R. Walls (London, 1964), ix-x and 1-12, and J.P.M. Swete, *Revelation* (Philadelphia, 1979), 41-42.

189 For the *Shepherd*, see Vision I.3, III.4-5, and Parable IX.13 (*SC* 53, 76-78, 108-112, and 318-322), and the comments of Joly, Ibid., 34-35. For Clement, see the *Excerpta ex Theodoto* 4.1-3, 5.3, 9, 11.1-14, and 12.1-2 (*SC* 23, 58-60, 62, 74-76, 80-82, and 82 resp.). For Gregory of Nyssa, the *Life of Moses* 14-18 (*SC* 1, 89-95). For Theodore of Mopsuestia, the *Commentary on the Lord's Prayer and on the Sacraments of Baptism and Eucharist*, trans. by A. Mingana, *Woodbrook Studies* 6 (1963), 79-95; and for Germanos, *On the Divine Liturgy* 1, 6-7, 16, 25, 37, and 41, trans. and text by P. Meyendorff (Crestwood, 1985), 56, 60, 74, 86, and 90-96.

first, emphasizes the sacraments, especially the Eucharist, as the "place" where heaven and earth meet, and it runs from St Irenaeus through the Cappadocians and the fourth- and fifth-century mystagogical writers.[190] The third line, embracing and employing the imagery of microcosm and macrocosm,[191] is later in developing. The great Origen's flawed attempt at a comprehensive Christian theology in the third century was couched almost entirely in terms of the Platonism of his day, and that included the notion of microcosm reflecting macro-cosm.[192] The latter is the principle which Origen justifies through his allegorical interpretation of Scripture and which enables him, for example, to see the soul's journey to God as mirrored in the history of Israel's progress through the desert to the land of promise.[193] Indeed, it frames his entire vision of man as a fallen spirit whose lowered estate not only reflects, but conditions God's creation of the physical world. The latter is for Origen thus both prison house and reform school. It is the merciful God's projection of a cosmos reflecting the fallen human condition and designed to lead our intellect (*nous*) back and up to

190 For Irenaeus, see *Adv.Haer.* IV.xvii.5 - xviii.6 (*SC* 100, pt. 2, 590-614; *ANF* I, 484-486). For the Cappadocians, see esp. Gregory of Nyssa, *Great Catechism* 33-37 (Srawley, 123-152; *Later Fathers*, 312-321). For the mystagogues, see Cyril of Jerusalem, *Lectures on the Christian Sacraments* I.8-9, II.7, and V.6 and 13 (Crestwood, 1977, rep. of SPCK, 1951), 15-16, 21, 32, and 35. Note also Ephrem of Syria and the "paradise mountain" as the Church in *Hymns on Paradise* (Crestwood, 1990), 52-55 and 88-96.

191 The term "microcosm" as a single word, however, dates back only to John of Damascus, *Ex.fid.* 26 (Kotter II, 76 and 79).

192 See Daniélou, *Origen*, trans. by W. Mitchell (New York, 1955), esp. 34-51, 153-172, 181-191, 210-218, and 294-308; also H. de Lubac, *Histoire et esprit: l'intelligence de l'écriture d'après Origène* (Paris, 1950), 346-354; R.P.C. Hanson, *Allegory and Event* (London, 1955), 276-281 and 355-356; and M. Harl, *Origène et la fonction révélatrice du Verbe incarné* (Paris, 1953), 93-95.

193 See *De prin.* II.1.3. and IV.3.9-13 (*SC* 252, 238-240 and *SC* 268, 374-392; for English, see *On First Principles*, trans. by Butterworth [New York, 1966], 78, and 301-310).

union with its creator.[194] Origen's scheme is further elaborated
by his fourth-century disciple, Evagrius, whom we touched on
above in connection with St Symeon on the ascetic life. For
Evagrius, as one scholar has observed, the different levels of
being represented by such terms as body, soul, intellect and
angel, signify in sum "moments of the knowledge of God," i.e.,
different stages in the ascent of the created spirit back to God
which His merciful Providence has seen fit to mirror in the
macrocosmos.[195]

Obviously, Origen's and Evagrius' scheme is "dis-incarna-
tional" in its fundamental inspiration. Taken to its logical
conclusions it would reduce both the Incarnation and the
Church of the sacraments to temporary expedients or stages on
the soul's way back to its original home. The process of
correcting Origen's (and Evagrius') system would preoccupy
the Christian East for centuries.[196] Two important contributors
to that process, and so to Symeon, were Maximus the Confessor and, before him, the mysterious author known as Dionysius
the Areopagite. The former has received quite a bit of attention
in this regard,[197] the latter very little.[198] Yet, while St Maximus'

194 See Ibid. II.1.1-5 and II.9-10 (*SC* 252, 244-5 and 352-95; Butterworth,
    76-80, and 129-146).
195 See *Kephalaia Gnostica* III.22, 28, 36-37, 47-51; IV.49, 51, 62; V.11;
    VI.20, 49, 59, and 75. See also D.B. Evans, *Leontius of Byzantium*
    (Washington, D.C., 1970), 89-111.
196 Like the hoary saying that all philosophy is a series of footnotes to
    Plato, so may roughly the same be said of Greek Christian theology
    with regard to Origen. See the opening lines of Meyendorff's summary
    of Eastern Christian doctrine in *Byzantine Theology*, 129ff.
197 Thus Sherwood, *The Earlier Ambigua*, and Thunberg, *Microcosm and
    Mediator*. The relationship of Maximus to Origen (and Origenism, i.e.,
    Evagrius in particular) has preoccupied, rightly, Maximian scholarship
    from its near beginnings this century.
198 The voices are few; see L. Bouyer, *The Spirituality of the New Testa-
    ment and the Fathers* (New York, 1982), 412-414, H. von Balthasar,
    Herrlichkeit II (Einsiedln, 1962), 147-214, and A. Golitzen, *Et Introibo
    ad Altare Dei* (Thessalonica, 1994).

little work, *The Mystagogy*,[199] comprises what is perhaps the
most admirable and lapidary statement of the fusion of mystical and ecclesial in patristic literature—at least until Nicolas
Cabasilas' *The Life in Christ* in the fourteenth century[200]—it is
from the work of the Areopagite that he drew in great part.[201]
It would be from the same source that Symeon in his turn
would take over three centuries after the Confessor. This is
rarely noted in the scholarship on the New Theologian, and
then only in connection with the antinomical or paradoxical
language the latter uses in connection with the mystical union.[202] But Dionysius is at least as important in his contribution
to our saint's understanding of the Church at worship.

For the Areopagite, the Church is at once our true world,
the foretaste of the world to come, the reflection of the heavenly liturgy, the milieu of our encounter with Christ, the body
of Christ and the image or icon of man redeemed.[203] The
different lines we spoke of just above meet and are joined. The
"centrifugal" dynamics of Origen and Evagrius, with respect
at least to the Church's altar, are adjusted in such a way as to
pull the believer into contemplation of the altar in order to
discover there the Incarnate Word Who, at the same time, is the
Reality encountered in the depths of his or her soul. Thus, for
example, Dionysius' famous illustration, borrowed from Gre-

199 *PG* 91, 657-717; for English, see *The Church, the Liturgy, and the Soul
    of Man*, trans. by J. Steed (Still River, Massachusetts, 1982), 59-119.
200 *PG* 150, 493-726; English by C. de Catanzaro, *The Life in Christ*
    (Crestwood, 1974). For Cabasilas' "sacramental mysticism," see Bo-
    briskoy, Ibid., 21-38.
201 So I would hold. See also R. Bornert, *Les commentaires byzantins de
    la Divine Liturgie: du VIIe au XVe siecle* (Paris, 1966), 87-104, and H.
    von Balthasar, *Kosmische Liturgie: Das Weltbild Maximus des Beken-
    ners* (Einsiedln, 1961), 313-329.
202 Thus see Darrouzès, *SC* 156, 50-51, 73, 79, and 114, note 1. See as well,
    Julien-Fraigneau, 172-181.
203 For the Church as world in Dionysius, see R. Roques, L'Univers
    Dionysien (Paris, 1954), esp. 36-134, and Golitzen, Et Introibo, 119-140.

gory of Nyssa, of the mystical ascent with the ascent of Moses
on Sinai is more than the rationalist exercise in apophatic
theology that some have taken it for.[204] It is as well a picture of
the Church at worship, and Moses is at once illustrative of the
soul at worship and a type of the Christian high priest celebrating the Liturgy.[205] After being purified, he ascends through
"many-voiced trumpets" and "lights" to "the place where God
is," and then "enters into the truly mystical darkness of un-
knowing."[206] While clearly a reference to Exodus 19, this
passage also recalls Christian worship, especially in its recollection of purification (as the Israelites at the foot of Sinai),
lights and sounds, and the hidden altar glimpsed through the
curtains which veil it—features of Syrian churches even in
Dionysius' day.[207] The connections between Christ, the
Church worshipping, the image of man, and the angels are
made explicit in the following passage from Dionysius' *Celestial Hierarchy:*

> Neither is it possible for the human intellect [nous] to
> be ranked with that immaterial imitation and contem-
> plation of the heavenly hierarchies [the angels] unless
> it make use of the material guide which is proper to it,
> and understand the visible beauties as reflections of the
> invisible splendor, the perceptible fragrances as impres-

---

204 *Mystical Theology* I.3 (Heil and Ritter, 143.18-144.15; Luibheid, 136-
137). For this passage as a purely rational exercise, see J. Vanneste, *Le
Mystère de Dieu* (Brussels, 1959), and the article by the same, "Is the
Mysticism of Dionysius Genuine?" *International Philosophical Quarterly* (1963): 286-300.

205 For Moses as a type of the Christian bishop, and the linkage of
Dionysius' Mystical Theology to his Ecclesiastical Hierarchy, see P.
Rorem, *Biblical and Liturgical Symbols in the Pseudo-Dionysian Syn-
thesis* (Toronto, 1984), esp. 140-142 and Golitzen, *Et Introibo*, 168-177.

206 *Myst.Theo.* I.3 (Heil and Ritter, 143; for English, Luibheid, 137).

207 See the "sacred veils" of *Divine Names* I.4 (Suchla, 114.2; Luibheid,
52); and for the role of the curtain in Syrian churches of the fourth-fifth
centuries, G. Schneider, "*Katapetasma*: Studien zum Ursprung liturgis-
cher Einselheiten östlicher Liturgien," *Kyrios* 1 (1936): 57-73.

sions of the spiritual [*noetos*] distribution, the material
lights an icon of the immaterial gift of light, the sacred
and extensive teaching [of the scriptures] [an image] of
the mind's intelligible fulfillment, the orders of the
ranks [of the clergy] here below [an icon] of the ordered
and harmonious orientation [hexis, literally "habit"] of
the mind toward what is divine, and the partaking of the
most divine Eucharist [an image] of participation in
Jesus.[208]

Our liturgy, Dionysius continues, imitates the angels and
makes us their "co-workers" and partakers of God.[209] The
physical elements of the Church's worship all convey a spiritual truth. The very ordering of the clergy comprise a suggestion of the well-ordered, i.e., virtuous, mind. All is icon, or
symbol, of a pervasive and unseen reality, summed up at the
end with the reference to the Eucharist and to Christ. Does this
mean that Dionysius holds a doctrine of the eucharistic presence which sees the latter as less than "real?" The point has
been debated by others,[210] but we would certainly see him as
very much like the New Theologian. Perhaps it would be better
to say that Symeon is very like the Areopagite: the bread is only
"bread" unless the unseen is perceived, just as divinity is
concealed in the Carpenter. That Symeon had read this passage
from the *Celestial Hierarchy* and admired it is evident, furthermore, from *Discourse* XIV.

In the latter, he takes up the question of the celebration of
the great feasts of the Church. The setting he appears to have
in mind is either the solemn commemoration of one of the
decisive moments in Christ's life—Nativity, Ascension, Pentecost, etc.—or else, perhaps, the veneration of Symeon the

208 *Celestial Hierarchy* I.3 (Heil and Ritter, 8; English, Luibheid, 137).
209 Ibid.
210 Cf. Rorem, *Symbolism*, 76-77, for the contra, and A. Louth, "Pagan
    Theurgy and Christian Sacramentalism in Denys the Areopagite," JTS 37
    (1986): 432-438, for the pro in reply to Rorem.

Pious, or of the monastery's altar feast or patron saint.[211] He
may indeed be looking in this discourse to set his struggle for
the glorification of his spiritual father in its proper perspective
by reminding his readers (and himself?) of the purpose and
meaning of liturgical worship. That purpose is nothing earthly.
"How," he asks, can the man who has "seen the Master" and
knows himself as "naked and poor"

> ...take pride in beauty, or exalt himself...or pay great
> attention to a multitude of candles and lamps, or fra-
> grances and perfumes, or an assembly of people, or a
> rich...table, or boast in the...presence of men who are
> glorious upon the earth?[212]

These things are all earthly, "here today and tomorrow gone."
The wise man therefore looks to what is not visible, "the future
[i.e., eschatological] events which are present in the rites being
celebrated," and will thus celebrate the feast "in the Holy
Spirit...with those who celebrate...in heaven."[213] No reckoning
of feasts or splendor in decoration suffices if one does not
realize that the latter do not comprise "the true feast, but are
symbols of the feast." Without that realization there is neither
"gain" nor "joy."[214]

Symeon certainly does not discourage liturgical solemni-
ties: "God forbid! On the contrary, I indeed both advise and
encourage you to do these things," but he does want to point
out how properly to do so and what the things done "in types
and symbols really mean."[215] In the process of this explanation
he also displays his debt to the Areopagite. The function, he
says, of the lamps in the church is "to show you the intelligible
light" (Dionysius' "immaterial gift of light"), and the fra-

211 *ED* XIV.49-53.
212 Ibid. 26-35.
213 Ibid. 35-44.
214 Ibid. 54-78.
215 Ibid. 87-89.

grances or incense used in the services "the intelligible myrrh," the anointing of the Spirit which "wells up from within" and "rises like sweet-smelling smoke"[216] (recall Dionysius' "spiritual distributions"). Symeon's further use of the *myron,* a sweet oil compounded of many perfumes, as reflecting the human composite, "composed and combined...with the spiritual perfume...the gifts...of the Spirit,"[217] also calls to mind Dionysius' description of the myron in his Ecclesiastical Hierarchy: Jesus is the "super-essential fragrance" Who pervades our being by virtue of the Incarnation.[218]

Stressing that our celebrations here-below are only "a type and shadow and symbol" of the heavenly feast to which we can neither add nor subtract,[219] Symeon shows nonetheless how we may participate in the celestial liturgy. He holds that each person must reflect the eternal celebration. Again, the Church at worship is the symbol or icon of the new man transfigured in Christ. His series of comparisons follows fairly closely the sequence quoted above from the *Celestial Hierarchy* and, like the latter, concludes with the Eucharist.[220] The lamps signify "that light by which the whole world of the virtues is completed," the perfumes and incense "the intelligible perfume of the Holy Spirit," the crowds of laity "the ranks of the holy angels," friends and dignitaries "all the saints," and the groaning board of refreshments "the living bread alone—not that which is perceptible and visible, but He Who comes to you in and through what is perceptible," and the wine "not...this visible wine, but that which appears as wine yet is perceived by the intellect as the blood of God, light inexpressible." The order is a little different from Dionysius'. The lights precede the perfumes, while crowds and dignitaries

216 Ibid. 93-121.
217 Ibid. 121-139.
218 *Eccl.Hier.* IV.3,4 (Heil and Ritter, 98-99; Luibheid, 228).
219 *ED* XIV.176-183.
220 Ibid. 144-223.

represent angels and saints rather than the order of clergy signifying the virtuous soul, but Symeon still appears clearly to be echoing the earlier writer. The thinking is also fundamentally the same. The worship of the Church connects us to the angels and to Christ while, at the same time, it reflects the soul in union with God. It also does more than simply reflect. It enables that union, accomplishes it, through the sacrament of communion. The latter, in Dionysius' phrase, is the icon or symbol of "participation in Jesus." Neither for him nor for Symeon does icon or symbol mean here a mere pointer or empty memorial. Rather, it conveys the presence which it signifies. It must be received "in perception and in knowledge," must be seen with the "intelligible eye of the soul."[221] For Dionysius it is the "sacrament of sacraments," that which, he tells his readers, illumined his own perception and allowed him to discern rightly all the meaning of the Christian mysteries.[222] Likewise, Symeon remarks at the end of this discourse that if one truly celebrates the feast and partakes worthily

> ...of the divine mysteries, all your life will be to you one single feast. And not a feast, but the beginning of a feast and a single Pascha, the passage and emigration from what is seen to what is sensed by the intellect, to that place where every shadow and type, and all the present symbols, come to an end...rejoicing eternally in the most pure sacrifice, in God the Father and co-essential Spirit, always seeing Christ and being seen by Him, ever being with Christ...than Whom nothing is greater in the Kingdom of God... Amen.[223]

221 Ibid. 224-247; compare with the phrase *hyp'hopsin* (into sight), in *Eccl.Hier*. III.3, 10, 12, and 13 (Heil and Ritter, 82-83, 89-90, 92-93; English, Luibheid, 213, 220, and 222); and to Dionysius' use of the verb *epigignosko* (to recognize), in *Eccl.Hier*. III.3,14 (Heil and Ritter, 82-83 and 93-94; English, Luibheid, 212-213 and 223).

222 *Eccl.Hier*. III.1 (Heil and Ritter, 81-82; English, Luibheid, 209).

223 *ED* XIV.180-193.

For Future Generations:
St. Symeon the Contributor

Ascetic, mystic, and theologian, prophet who excoriated the hierarchy of his day and simultaneously held the priesthood in highest esteem, ferocious opponent and tender shepherd, builder of communities and advocate of poverty, preacher of God's transcendence and convinced of His immanence, worshipper at the altar of the Church and celebrant of the mystery revealed in the heart, singer of the Word made flesh and manifested in the light of the Spirit, St. Symeon was himself a bundle of paradoxes. No systematic theologian he, but as certainly a theologian in that he united in his own person the tradition of the fathers and revealed it to others as one living truth. Nothing is new in his writings, at least in the sense of a new doctrine or "creative" adaptation to the needs of the times. He is utterly faithful to the teachings of the councils and fathers and, what is more, understands them so well that they become part and parcel of himself and of his world. He lives and moves and breathes the scriptures, the liturgy, and the ascetic writings. He explains himself and his experiences wholly in their context. If there is anything new in him, it is his tone, his personal witness that the Church's dogmas and worship communicate a reality, *the* reality, and that one may—rather, must—partake of it in this life. While he certainly departs from custom in citing his own encounters with God, even here he can and does point to a precedent in the Apostle Paul, and refuses to acknowledge any difference between the latter's experience and his own. In that last, i.e., in his insistence on a continuum of experience, we may discern a characteristic emphasis not only of Symeon, but of the whole Eastern Church. Concerning the activity of the Holy Spirit now as in the days of the Apostles, Symeon's earliest modern commentator, Karl Holl, sees a fundamental difference between the Eastern and Western Churches. He is worth citing at length:

> In the Western view the apostolic era is the classically productive time. Subsequently the Spirit, though never separated from the Church, has only the task of keeping that inheritance pure and unsullied. . . . The Greek view, to the contrary, is that the Spirit lives on, not as merely providing assurance for [religious] knowledge and [ecclesiastical] institutions, but rather as creative. The inheritance is, to some extent, created anew from generation to generation.[1]

Like all generalizations, this one, too, breaks down somewhat on closer inspection. Attitudes which Holl defines here as characteristically "western" have always had a role to play in the Eastern Church. They began, in fact, to play an entirely predominant role in Byzantine church life not long after Symeon's death and, had it not been for the hesychast movement in the fourteenth century, it is possible that what Holl thinks peculiarly "eastern," would have survived only on the fringes of Orthodoxy, if at all, or in break-away sects surrounding it like a kind of penumbra such as we find, for example, in the varied expressions of the "Old Belief" in eighteenth- and nineteenth-century Russia. Following the death in the 1090's A.D. of his disciple, Nicetas Stethatos, the New Theologian appears to have fallen into a kind of oblivion, only to experience a "resurrection" centuries later as a champion of the Hesychast monks of Mt. Athos, whose "victory meant at the same time the canonization of his theology."[2]

1   Holl, 221, note 1.

2   Völker, *Praxis*, 489, and Holl, 30 and 222-223.

But why should any such "resurrection" have been necessary if Symeon was truly the faithful witness to biblical and
patristic thought that we have sought to present? The answer, so
far as one may speak of "answers" in an historical survey, lies
in the to and fro between the polarities we have noted at various
points in this essay, polarities which reflect the tensions inherent
in the life of the Church as "in" the world yet not "of" it. Holl
was right to identify the "pneumatic" and "charismatic" thrust
of the New Theologian as a traditional—not to say fundamental—aspect of the Eastern Church. On the other hand, any kind
of continuity down the centuries of life "in" the world requires
the structures of an institution, i.e., hierarchy, law, recognized
authority. In the context of Symeon's world, law and order in
the Church were provided by the ranks of clergy headed by the
bishops and presided over by the patriarch. The episcopacy in
turn understood itself as the guardian of the single true faith of
the Christian Roman Empire headed by the "sacred emperor."[3]
Church and empire were complementary facets of a single
organism, one sacred polity, and Byzantine churchmen were
not slow to remind their charges of this when necessary, as the
letter of the Patriarch Antony to Grand Duke Basil of Moscow,
sixty years before the empire's fall, amply demonstrates.[4] The
historically conditioned nature of the Church's relationship
with the Roman Empire and the dangers posed to the faith by
this intimate bond were scarcely realized by anyone during the
long life of Byzantium though, as we have seen, Symeon does
seem to have had some sense of the contradictions implicit in
honoring imperial power as the mainstay of the Gospel of the
Crucified: "if it is difficult for a rich man, how shall a ruler ever
enter [the kingdom of heaven]? Never!"[5] It is thus surely no

3   See Hussey, *Church and Learning*, 117-137.

4   Taken from D. Obolensky, *The Byzantine Commonwealth* (London,
    1974), 342-343.

5   EDI III.601-602.

accident that his message comes to the fore only after the
disasters of the thirteenth and fourteenth centuries—crusaders,
Turks, and civil wars—had fatally weakened the power of the
state. Certainly, the Church hierarchy continued to cling to the
office of the emperor as symbolic point of unity of the Orthodox *ecumene* long after its actual power had been reduced to a
distant memory, but this reflex cannot disguise the fact that the
real leadership of the Orthodox had changed hands.[6] It was
more truly vested in the patriarchs of Constantinople, men in
turn shaped by a Hesychast revival which "had its effects far
beyond the shrinking boundaries of the Byzantine Empire . . .
[and had] lit up the whole Orthodox world."[7]

The foundations of state power had not, however, been
shaken in the New Theologian's own day. Although "almost
all the major themes of the later hesychasts can be discovered
in his writings,"[8] and although manuscript evidence alone
bears witness that these were a primary source of inspiration
for the fourteenth-century monks of Athos who led the revival,[9] they were still obliged to lie fallow for over two
hundred years. During his own lifetime Symeon was swim-
ming against the tide. Byzantium of the eleventh and twelfth
centuries was still a powerful state, and the influence of the
state authorities, particularly the dominance of the emperors
over their bishops and patriarchs, reached a kind of apogee
during the reigns of the three Comnene emperors who ruled
from 1081 to 1185.[10] As might be expected from devout but
still autocratic rulers, this period was marked by a predominant
emphasis on order in the Church and a corresponding distrust

---

6   See D.M. Nicol, *Church and Society in the Last Centuries of Byzantium*
     (Cambridge, 1977), 3-28; and the illuminating study by J. Meyendorff,
     Byzantium and the Rise of Russia (Crestwood, 1989), esp. 96-118.

7   Nicol, *Church and Society*, 88.

8   McGuckin, *Chapters*, 24-25.

9   See note 55, page 136 above.

10   Hussey, 142ff.

of the "wild card" element represented by the traditional figure of the charismatic holy man. To be fair, the authorities had a case. Byzantine monasticism was nothing if not unruly, highly litigious, and frequently tainted by scandals.[11] Charismaticism had always posed the danger—and usually the fact—of fanaticism and spiritual quackery. The eleventh and twelfth centuries signaled a particularly marked swing of the pendulum toward the assertion of ecclesiastical (and thus state) authority. In this respect, Stephen of Nicomedia was much more typical of the age than was Symeon. The twelfth century was, in both Latin West and Greek East, the great era of codification and commentary on the church canons.[12] In the greatest of the Byzantine canonists, Theodore Balsamon, we find a clear impatience with claims to a charismatic authority on the part of unordained monks, and with regard in particular to just those issues Symeon raises in his *Letter on Confession.*[13]

The pendulum swung very far, indeed. The twelfth century is marked by "an increasing, official intolerance of the holy man's kind of holiness."[14] The great charismatic figures of the past were seen as precisely that, i.e., as belonging to a past which was complete and therefore closed to any who, like Symeon, sought to claim that sanctity was not confined to a distant golden age.[15] It was an atmosphere which would prove even less kind to those who followed in the New Theologian's footsteps than it had to Symeon himself. The condemnation by the patriarchal chancery on charges of heresy of Theodore of Blachernae (ca. 1085) and Constantine Chrysomallos (Spring, 1140) bear witness to an abiding hostility on the part of high

11 Ibid. 158-181, and also Amand de Mendieta, *Garden of the Panagia,* 80-81.
12 See Meyendorff, *Byzantine Theology,* 85-86.
13 See Paul Magdalinos, "The Byzantine Holy Man," 59-60, and Holl, 291-301.
14 Ibid. 64.
15 Ibid. 61-62.

Byzantine churchmen to the emphases characteristic of the New Theologian. While it is possible to suspect that both men may have pushed Symeon's thought too far in the direction of a uniquely charismatic authority,[16] it is even clearer that neither preached the sort of heresy—dualist bogomilism or "Messalianism"—that the court found in them. As one scholar has observed,

> . . . the censors could have taken practically the same excuses for condemnation from the works of Symeon. To opt for a coincidence of doctrines would be abusive, while to deny that both the one [Symeon] and the others refer to a single type of charismatic—or, if you prefer, of inspired—religion would be even more so.[17]

The "whole intellectual context" of the men so condemned postulates instead "the inner transformation of man in the spirit of the Eastern Christian doctrine of deification."[18] Neither is there any evidence in the sources of any stance taken by these men against episcopal authority *per se*.[19] What appears instead from these trials is a position taken in direct and perhaps conscious opposition to the New Theologian's characteristic themes. The latter is, in any case, the one "significant absence in the series" of persons condemned.[20] That he was not himself condemned was almost certainly due, as we noted above, to his personal influence at court and circle of influential friends and disciples, including Nicetas, who lived on until the end of the eleventh century and had certainly led the movement to canonize Symeon. The authorities, however, appeared bound and determined to prevent any re-occurrence of the influence exercised by this "crazy zealot." In the main, as evidenced by the virtual eclipse of the New Theologian's name and writings (the

16 Gouillard, "Quatre Procès," 28 and 33-37.

17 Ibid. 28.

18 Milan Loos, *Dualist Heresy*, 97.

19 Gouillard, "Quatre Procès," 45.

20 Ibid.

loss, for example, of the service in his honor written by Nicetas) for over two hundred years, they appear to have won a temporary victory.

But it was an illusory victory. The very fact of the trials of Theodore and Chrysomallos indicate a lively, if underground, continuity of the New Theologian's thought. Chrysomallos, in fact, seems to have been associated with the partial composition of the *Orations* which for long circulated under the name of Symeon.[21] The bishops of the patriarchal chancery were thus in all likelihood "engaging themselves in battle with a legion."[22] "They could not," says Jean Gouillard, "have been more mistaken. . . . There would always be emulators of the New Theologian . . . who would reckon that the mandate of the Spirit was worth at least as much as a bishop's imprimatur."[23] Symeon may have disappeared from the official church for a time, but we may be confident that his memory and his works continued to be quietly cherished by other circles, monastic and lay, to await their open vindication by the conscience of the universal Church.

That day came with the hesychast revival. Its main spokesman, St. Gregory Palamas, does not, it is true, openly cite the New Theologian as an authority on a par with the "fathers," i.e., with such as "Macarius" or especially St. Maximus the Confessor.[24]

---

21 See Gouillard, "Constantine Chrysomallos," 313-327, and Krivocheine, "Writings," 305-312, on the inferior quality of the "Orations" circulated under Symeon's name. Gouillard holds Chrysomallos out as the compiler and, to a degree, the author. These were in turn later on, in nineteenth-century Russia, what Theophan the Recluse translated into that language. The English-speaking reader can find a sample of Chrysomallos' editing available in *The Sin of Adam and our Redemption: Seven Homilies by St. Symeon the New Theologian* put out by the St. Herman's Brotherhood (Platina, California, 1979). These, typically, mingle elements from both the *Catecheses* and the *Ethical Discourses*.

22 Gouillard, *Chrysomallos*, 37.

23 Ibid.

24 Krivocheine, *Light*, 393, note 4.

Perhaps it was the case that a sort of cloud of controversy still hung over Symeon, dating back to the heresy trials of the twelfth century and the rumor-mongering that had gone on during the saint's own lifetime. Yet St. Gregory did express admiration for him[25] and, more importantly, while he does not name his source, he quotes from Symeon's works. We have already noted one such instance above. Another and striking case occurs early in Palamas' major work, *The Triads in Defense of the Holy Hesychasts.* Here we find St. Gregory arguing in favor of the experience of God as light and appealing to II Corinthians 12:2-4 as his proof text. In an analysis of this text which also alludes to an episode in the *Life* of St. Benedict of Nursia,[26] Gregory makes clear use of Symeon's argument in *Discourse* III below. St. Paul is taken as paradigm of the mystical experience, his experience in the rapture to the "third heaven" is seen as a vision of the light of the world to come, and the Apostle's "ineffable speech" is identified with sight.[27]

St. Symeon thus came into his own. The Hesychast Councils of the 1340s and 50s effectively placed the seal of official Orthodox Church recognition on his life's witness by upholding the teaching of St. Gregory. It was a long time in coming

25 *Triades* I.2.12, ed. by Meyendorff (Louvain, 1959), 99-101.

26 See E. Lanne, "L'Interprétation palamite."

27 *Triades* I.iii.5 and 21-22 (Meyendorff, 115-119 and 153-157); for English, *Gregory Palamas, the Triads,* trans. by N. Gendle (New York, 1983), 34 and 38-39. See Meyendorff's note 18, page 122, referring to Maximus' use of *II Cor.* 12 in *PG* 91.1076BC and 1114C. What is peculiar in Palamas' use of St. Paul's "ineffable speech" here, though, is his equating it to a vision of light, i.e., just what we find in Symeon in *ED* III.247-309, and not in Maximus. We incline thus to the opinion that the doctor of hesychasm had Symeon in mind when he wrote these passages, linking them further to the vision of the ray of light embracing the universe from the *Life of Benedict.* Lanne as well seems to lean to this view, although he does not mention *ED* III specifically (Lanne, "L'Interprétation palamite," 31-36 and 38). Lanne's references are to "George's" vision and the *Life* of Symeon, *Vie* 8-10 and 92-96. He makes no specific use of Symeon's own treatment of *II Cor.* 12.

and, in subsequent centuries, both he and hesychasm would suffer eclipse—or even condemnation—in different parts of the Orthodox world.[28] The monks of Athos, however, would not forget. Twice since the fourteenth century, in the eighteenth and again in the twentieth centuries, his vision as confirmed by Palamas would re-surface to invigorate the Orthodox world.[29] But none of this is to say that the New Theologian was doing anything other than articulating, or witnessing to, the testimony of the scriptures and tradition before him. His was a relatively lonely voice in eleventh-century Byzantium, but was surely nonetheless a most authoritative expression of the faith: the Spirit of God at work in the Apostles is alive in the Church of every generation, offering the same assurance and taste of the Kingdom to come as was afforded to Peter and Paul and the others of the Twelve.

We would like to close this introduction to St. Symeon with an observation made a hundred years ago about the great work which first advertised monastic life to a newly-converted empire, St. Athanasius' *Life of Antony*. The quotation speaks as much about Symeon as it does about the "father of monks."

28 See Krivocheine, *Light* 391

29 That the essentials of Symeon's witness, as summed up in the distinctive teachings of hesychasm, survived in the Orthodox world—at least on Mt. Athos—is testified to by the English-speaking visitors who have recorded their journeys to the Holy Mountain, beginning with John Covell in the 1660s. *The Journal of John Covell*, with notes by F.W. Hasluck, in *The Annual of the British School at Athens* XVII (1910/11), 111. The sequence continues with Lord Curzon in the early nineteenth, *Visits to the Monasteries of* the *Levant* (Ithaca, New York, 1955, rep. of 1849 ed.), 341-343; then A. Riley in the 1880s, *Athos or the Mountain of the Monks* (London, 1897), 193-197; R. Byron in the 1920s, *The Station, Athos* (London, 1936), 155-175; S. Loch in the 50s, *Athos: The Holy Mountain* (London, 1957), 207-208, and P. Sherrard in the 80s, *Athos: The Holy Mountain* (Woodstock, New York, 1982), 148-171. The dogmatic traces, i.e., Symeon as reflected in the formal statements of the hierarchy, are harder to find—at least until after St. Nicodemus in the late eighteenth century.

Karl Holl is comparing (rather unfairly) the work of Clement of Alexandria to the later book by Athanasius:

> . . . how far it is still from his [Clement's] abstract expressions . . . to the simple, intuitive, living picture of the *Vita Antonii*! Could this progress, the representation of the ideal in a real person, have been possible without there having appeared in the meantime men who had actually embodied the ideal in themselves?[30]

---

30 Holl, 146, note 1.

Appendix

We have taken the text of St. Symeon's *Letter on Confession* from the critical edition compiled and printed first by Karl Holl in the latter's *Enthusiamus und Bussgewalt*, 110-127, and reprinted recently in the edition of Symeon's complete works published by Orthodox Kpyseli (Thessalonica, 1990), vol. III, 423-439. Although some have raised doubts recently about the authenticity of this essay (see the discussion by K.T. Ware in the latter's "Forward" to *Spiritual Direction in the Ancient Christian East*, esp. note 18, page xxix), we find no difficulty in accepting it as the New Theologian's own. It is certainly representative of his thought, even if not—perhaps (and only perhaps)—from his own hand.

The "Epistle" begins with the question whether or not only ordained clergy have the authority to "bind and loose" from sins. After protesting his unworthiness to probe the things of God, Symeon proceeds to develop his thesis that "binding and loosing" is a charismatic gift. He dwells first on the necessity of confession for everyone. All have broken the commandments of God at some time and all are therefore in need at some time of an intercessor, a physician and friend of God, who will show them how they may be reconciled to the God Whose mercies (i.e., the saving works of Christ) they have spurned. No one, however, may presume to the office of intercessor without having first been reconciled himself or herself to God. This is the familiar key to Symeon's subsequent development of a theory of "apostolic succession." While it was to the twelve that Christ first gave the divine authority to "bind and loose" from sins (Symeon cites John 20:22-23), and while no one questioned that it was to the bishops as successors of the Apostles that the authority was handed on at first, it is the sad truth that the bishops and, following them, the priests "made themselves strangers to it" by falling prey to the lures of the devil and becoming corrupt. To be sure, he adds, bishops and priests still have the authority to celebrate the sacraments (*hierourgein*), but they no longer necessarily have the personal authority to intercede with God on behalf of others (he does not, though, rule out at least the possibility of some holy men among the clergy). Thus this authority devolved upon the "elect," by whom Symeon specifies that he means the monks. Not all of them, certainly, since they, too, have often been spoiled by the same corrupting power as has soiled the clergy, but he leaves little doubt that, however rare they may be, God's friends and our intercessors are chiefly to be found among the ascetics. He concludes by offering the example of his own experience of his elder, Symeon the Pious, and asks his readers to beg God with tears, constantly, that they may be led to one of His holy ones and so be reconciled with Him.

LETTER ON CONFESSION

1. Dear Father and Brother,

His Unworthiness

You have asked our worthlessness to reply to your question: "Is it really permissible to confess one's sins to monks who are not priests?" and then you added the following: "Since we hear that [the authority] to bind and loose has been given exclusively to the priests." This is undoubtedly an edifying question, and it speaks well of your fiery longing and godly fear. While we have accepted your intention as a good one, since you are trying to learn about matters which are divine and sacred, we are not ourselves equipped either to make such distinctions or to write about them. We would therefore have preferred to keep silent. To interpret spiritual things by the spiritual [see I Cor 2:13] is for men who are holy and dispassionate, and in way of life, in word and in virtues, we are very far from such holiness.

2. However, since it is written that "The Lord is near to all who call upon Him in truth" [Ps 145:18], I, too, who am unworthy, have called upon the Same, and I will speak to you about these matters—though not with my own words, but with the divine and God-inspired Scripture itself. It is not I who will be doing the teaching. I shall instead be presenting you with Scripture's own witness concerning the issues you have raised. By God's grace, I shall thus preserve both myself and my listeners from a double precipice: that of the man who hid his talent, and that other of the person who unworthily and vaingloriously—indeed, with a darkened mind—sets himself up as an expert in divine teachings.

Where can our discourse make a better beginning than with Him Who is the beginning of all things and is Himself without beginning? This is surely the better way. It insures that what we have to say will be sure and certain. We were not created by the angels, nor have we learned from men. Rather, we have been mystically taught by the Wisdom from on high, indeed by the grace which comes through the Spirit. So do we always and at every hour continue to be taught. Calling upon that same Wisdom, let us proceed by setting out first of all the manner of confession and its power.

The Definition of Confession and its Necessity

3. Confession is nothing other than the necessary avowal or recognition of one's own failings and foolishness, that is, a realization of one's poverty. As the Lord says in the Gospel parable: "A certain creditor," He says, "had two debtors: one owed him five hundred denarii and the other fifty. When they

could not pay, he forgave them both" [Lk 7:41-42]. Every believer is thus a debtor with respect to his true master and God. He is also going to be held to account for what he has received at the throne of God's dread and terrible judgment where all of us, emperors and poor men alike, shall stand naked and bowed down before Him. Consider everything that He has given to us. While these gifts are so numerous that no one could count all of them, still the greater and more perfect are: our deliverance from condemnation, our sanctification from pollution, our procession out of darkness toward His inexpressible light, our having become His children and sons and heirs through divine Baptism, our being clothed with God Himself, our becoming His members and our reception of the Holy Spirit to dwell within us—the royal seal with Whom the Lord brands those sheep who are His own—and finally (but how much else I might add!) His making us like Himself and creating us His brothers and co-heirs. All these, and others still greater than these, holy Baptism grants immediately to everyone who is baptized. These gifts are what the divine Apostle called God's wealth and inheritance [see Col 1:12; Eph. 3:8; 2 Cor 4:7].

All the Commandments are Necessary: the "Bodyguards" of Grace

4. The Lord's commandments are like guardians of these ineffable gifts and benefits. They surround the believer and the treasure stored up inside his soul like a kind of wall, keeping both of them safe and preventing any thief or enemy from laying hands on them. We, however, fancy that we are ourselves the guardians of the loving God's commandments, and as a result feel ourselves greatly burdened. We ignore the fact that it is instead we who are guarded by them, since the person who keeps God's commandments does not protect them so much as himself. He protects himself thus from the visible and invisible adversaries whom Paul

made clear are dreadful and innumerable when he said:

> For we are not contending with flesh and blood, but
> against the principalities, against the powers, against
> the world rulers of the darkness of this age, against the
> spiritual beings of wickedness in the heavenly
> places . . . [Eph. 6:12]

These are clearly the spirits of the air who have always been invisibly arrayed against us.

Therefore, whoever guards the commandments is guarded by them and does not lose the wealth which God has entrusted to him. Whoever despises them, however, finds himself naked and easily overcome by his enemies and, having lost all that wealth, becomes answerable to the King and Master for everything that we mentioned above. For a human being to give such an account, or to find those things for himself, is impossible. They belong to heaven, and to Him Who came down from heaven—and daily comes down—to distribute and apportion them to the faithful. Where then could those who received and then lost them be able to find them again? Truly, nowhere at all! Neither was Adam nor any of his sons able to effect his own restoration or that of any of his descendants. Not until the God Who transcends nature had become his [Adam's] son according to the flesh, our Lord Jesus Christ, Who, when He had come, raised both Adam and ourselves from the Fall by His divine power. The person who thinks he does not need to keep all of the commandments, but can keep some while neglecting others, should realize that if he neglects just one of them he will forfeit everything.

Let me give an example. Imagine that the commandments are represented by twelve armed men and that these are arrayed in a circle. You stand in the middle, naked, but protected by these soldiers. Next, imagine that there are still other soldiers advancing against the twelve from all sides, opposing warriors who are attacking and trying to lay hold on you so that they can slaughter you immediately. If in this case one of the twelve were, by his own will, to drop away from the formation and neglect his custody, and so leave his spot like an open door to the adversary, what then would the advantage be of having the other eleven when one of the enemy had slipped in among them and cut you to pieces because the guards were unable to come to your assistance? While they might want to turn around and help you, they cannot because they would in that case themselves be destroyed by their assailants. The same thing will certainly happen to you if you do not keep the commandments. For once you have been wounded by just one enemy and fall down, all the commandments will abandon you, and then after a little while all your strength will be taken from you as well.

Let me put it another way. Imagine a jar filled with wine or oil. Unless the jar remains completely intact—that is, if some hole should appear in it at any point—all its contents will slowly leak away. In just this way if you fall away by negligence even a little from one of the commandments, you fall away from all the rest. It is just as Christ says: "To the one who has will more be given and he will have abundance; but from him who has not, even what he thinks he has will be taken away" [Mt 25:29]; and again: "Whoever relaxes one of these commandments"—obviously, by "relaxes" here He means "transgresses"—"and teaches men so, shall be called least in the Kingdom of Heaven" [Mt 5:19]. And Paul also says: "Whatever overcomes a man, to that he is enslaved" [2 Pet. 2:19]; and again: "The sting of death is sin" [I Cor 15:56]. He does not mean "this sin" or "that sin," but that whatever sin it might be, it is the sting of death. He calls sin death's sting because those who are stung by it die. Every sin leads to death. As the same Apostle says: "Once a man has sinned, he has already died" [Rom 6:10, misquoted]. Such a man has become subject to debt and sin, and the thieves have left him for dead lying on the roadside [see Lk 10:30].

Once Fallen, the Sinner Must Seek an Intermediary

5. So what else does a man who is dying want, unless it is to be raised up again; or a debtor without means to repay, unless it is to receive remission of his debt, lest he be thrown into prison until he make good on his obligation? Indeed, seeing how the latter has nothing, he will never escape from the everlasting darkness of his jail. Just so will the man who has been broken by the spiritual thieves look for a sympathetic and compassionate physician to come minister to him. He no longer has the fear of God burning inside him and forcing him to go looking for the doctor himself. Instead, having unstrung the power of his soul because of his contempt, he lies as a terrible and pitiable spectacle for everyone who can see clearly—or better, spiritually—into those failures which are proper to the soul. Because of his sin he has become the devil's slave—for, says Paul, "Do you not know . . . you are slaves of the one whom you obey, whether of righteousness which leads to righteousness, or of lawlessness which leads to lawlessness?" [Rom 6:16]. He has become a thing of mockery to God the Father, something to be trampled on by the adversaries who are apostate to God. He is left stripped of the robe of royal purple. He has been blackened, left a child of the devil rather than of God. What can he do in order to arrive again at possession of those things from which he has fallen away? Obviously, he will look for an intercessor and friend of God, someone capable of restoring him to his former state and reconciling him to God the Father. For the man who has once been joined to Christ by grace and has become His member and been adopted by him, if this man should by abandoning Him return like a dog to his vomit [2 Pet 2:22] by, for example, being joined to a sinful woman or to some other body, he shall be condemned with the unbelievers as having dishonored and insulted Christ. According to the Apostle, "We are Christ's

body and individually members of it" [I Cor 12:27]. So whoever entwines himself with a harlot makes the member of Christ's body the member of a harlot [see I Cor 6:15], and, since whoever has practiced such things has outraged his Master and God, he cannot be reconciled with Him except by means of someone else who is an intercessor and holy, a friend and servant of Christ, and by departing from evil.

6. Let us therefore flee first of all from sin. If, though, we are wounded by its arrows, then let us not waste time by letting the sin's venom grow sweet in us like honey. Neither, like a wounded bear, should we make the injury worse by worrying at it. Let us run instead directly to the spiritual physician and vomit up the venom of sin through confession and spit out its poison. Let us receive the penances he assigns us as an antidote, and always strive to fulfill them with a warm faith and in the fear of God. All who have emptied themselves completely of the wealth entrusted to them, who have dissipated their father's inheritance with harlots and publicans, whose conscience is so inclined downwards by their great shame that they are unable to look upwards because they have lost their freedom to speak to God boldly, all such people naturally seek out a man of God to stand as sponsor for their debt in order that, through him, they may approach God.

I think it is impossible for anyone to be reconciled with God without making a sincere and labored repentance. Never has anyone heard, nor has it ever been written in the God-inspired scriptures, that anyone could accept the sins of another or give an account of them without the sinner having first provided the evidence of worthy fruits of repentance, fruits which are proportionate to the form of his sin, and laying down his own labors as a foundation. So says the voice of the Word's Forerunner: "Bear fruit that befits repentance and do not presume to say to yourselves, 'We have Abraham as our father'"

[Mt 3:8-9]. Our Lord Himself spoke as follows about those who conduct themselves senselessly: "Amen I say to you, even if Moses and Daniel should arise in order to choose out their sons and daughters, they shall in no wise be chosen" [Jer 14:14-16, LXX]. So what should we do, what should we who wish to repent contrive for the remission of our debt and our recall from disaster? Listen, and with God's help I will settle the question for you.

The Spiritual Father, a True Physician

7. Seek out one who is, if you will, an intercessor, physician, and a good counselor. A good counselor, that he may propose ways of repentance which agree with good advice. A physician, that he may prescribe medicine which is appropriate for each of your wounds, and finally an intercessor, that he may propitiate God by standing before Him face to face and offering Him prayer and intercession on your behalf. Do not go and try to find some flatterer or slave to his belly and make him your counselor and ally lest, accommodating himself to your will and not to what God wants, he teach you what you want to hear and leave you in reality an unreconciled enemy. Nor should you choose an inexperienced physician lest, by extreme severity and untimely operations and cauterizations, he plunge you into the depths of despair or—and this is the worst possible course—allow you by inappropriate sympathy to think you are getting better when in fact you are still ailing, and so deliver you over to what you had hoped to avoid, I mean to eternal punishment. For this course of action does no more than furnish us with the illness that is already killing the soul.

As for an intercessor and friend of God—that, I think, is not quite so easily to be found. "For not all who are descended from Israel are Israelites" [Rom 9:6]. Such men are instead those who both own the name and have clearly understood the name's force, that is, an intellect which looks upon God [see Gen 32].

Neither are all who call upon the name of Christ truly Christians: "For not everyone who says to Me 'Lord, Lord,'" says Christ, "shall enter the Kingdom of Heaven, but he who doest the will of my Father" [Mt 7:21]; and likewise He says:

> Many who say to Me, 'Lord, Lord, did we not cast out demons in Your name?'; and I will say to them: 'Amen I say to you, I do not know you. Depart from Me, you workers of iniquity' [Mt 7:22-23 and 25:13].

Not an Office to Presume to Fill: Example of Imperial Court

8. We must, my brothers, therefore be careful on this account, both those of us who intercede and those who have sinned and wish to be reconciled, in order that neither those who intercede draw down wrath upon themselves rather than reward, nor that those who have offended and are striving earnestly to be reconciled chance to encounter a hostile and murderous and evil counselor in place of an intercessor. The evil counselors will hear a terrible warning: "Who set you up as rulers and judges of My people?" and again: "Hypocrite, first take the log out of your own eye, and then you will see clearly to take the speck out of your brother's eye" [Mt 7:5]. "Log" here means some passion or lust which obscures the eye of the soul. And, in the same vein: "Physician, heal yourself" [Lk 4:23]; and again:

> But to the sinner God says: "What right have you to recite My statutes, or take up My covenant with your mouth? For you have hated discipline, and you have cast My words behind you" [Ps 50:16-17].

Paul, too, says:

> Who are you to pass judgment on the servant of another? It is before his own master that he stands or falls. God is capable by means of His faithful servant of making him stand [Rom 14:4].[1]

1   Symeon alters the second half of the text.

9. Brothers and Fathers! In light of the above, I shudder and tremble. I beseech all of you, securing myself as well by means of this prayer to you, that you not conduct yourselves contemptuously with regard to these mysteries. They are holy and terrible for everyone concerned. Do not play with things that are not toys, nor let any of this be held against our souls by reason of our vainglory, or love of praise, or insensitivity, or hope of gain—for it does happen that strange, tempting thoughts come over people when they are called "Rabbi" or "Father." Let us not, I repeat, let us not shamelessly reach for the dignity of the Apostles, but rather be instructed by the following example of life in the world.

If someone had the audacity to make himself out to be the representative of the earthly emperor and were convicted of secretly holding and doing those things which are entrusted to that office, or indeed were subsequently to announce and practice it openly, both he and his co-conspirators and subordinates would be subject to the most extreme penalties as an example to others. What, then, will surely happen in future to those who snatch unworthily at the rank of the Apostles?

10. You should not want to become intercessors for others before you have yourself been filled with the Holy Spirit, or before you know, by perceiving in your soul, that you are loved as a friend by the King of all. Not everyone who knows the earthly emperor is able to intercede with him for others. They are exceedingly few who are able to do this. Out of their own virtue, and sweat, and labors they are able to speak boldly before him. Such people have no need of intercessors themselves. They speak together with the emperor person to person.[2] Fathers and brothers, shall we not then be careful of this rank for God's sake? Shall we not honor the heavenly King at least as much as the earthly emperor? Or shall we instead snatch at and grant ourselves title to the thrones at His right hand and at

2   Literally, "mouth to mouth."

his left before we have asked for and received them? Oh, the audacity! How great a shame would then lay hold of us?! Because, unless we were condemned as well on some other count, for this cause alone we would be dishonorably deprived of enthronement as convicted of contempt and would then be thrown out into the unquenchable fire.

But, let this suffice as a warning. Let all pay close heed to themselves. Indeed, it is just for this reason, that is, as a warning, that we have made this extended digression. Now then, my child, let us speak to the question you asked us at the beginning.

Monks May Confess Us: Decline of Episcopacy and Priesthood

11. It is permissible for an unordained monk to confess us. You will find this to be the case everywhere. This is because of the vesture and likeness [*proschema*] given by God as the monk's inheritance and by which monks are named. So is it written in the God-inspired writings of the Fathers, and you will find this to be the case should you chance to examine them. To be sure, prior to the monks only the bishops had that authority to bind and loose which they had received in succession to the Apostles. But, when time had passed and the bishops had become useless, this dread authority passed on to priests of blameless life and worthy of divine grace. Then also, when the latter had become polluted, both priests and bishops becoming like the rest of the people with many—just as to-day—tripped up by spirits of deceit and by vain and empty titles and all perishing together, it was transferred, as we said above, to God's elect people, I mean to the monks. It was not that it had been taken away from the priests and bishops, but rather that they had made themselves strangers to it. "For every priest is appointed a mediator [between] God and men by God," says Paul, "and is bound to offer sacrifice as much for the people as for himself" [Heb 5:1-3, paraphrased].

Christ is the Source of the Authority to Bind and Loose

12. But let us take up our discourse at an earlier point and see from when, and how, and to whom this power of celebrating the sacraments [*hierourgein*] and of binding and loosing was given from the beginning, and so proceed in due order just as you asked the question so that the solution may be clear, not just for you but for everyone else. When our Lord and God and Savior said to the man who had the withered hand, "Your sins are forgiven you," the Hebrews in attendance were all saying: "This man is blaspheming. Who can forgive sins except for God alone?" [see Mt 9:3; Mk 2:7; Lk 5:21]. Up to that time remission of sins had not yet been granted, not to prophets, nor to priests, nor to any of the patriarchs. The scribes were thus making difficulties because, really, a kind of strange, new teaching and reality was being proclaimed. And, because of this newness and strangeness, the Lord did not find fault with them. Instead, He taught them what they were ignorant of by proving that it was as God and not as man that He granted remission of sins. For He says to them: "But that you may know that the Son of Man has authority to forgive sins" [Mt 9:6], He says to the man with the withered hand, "Stretch out your hand," and he stretched it out and it was restored "whole, healthy like the other" [Mt 12:13]. By means of this visible wonder He provided a guarantee of the greater and invisible one. The same applies to Zaccheus [Lk 19:1ff], to the harlot [Lk 7:36f], to Matthew at his tax collector's post [Mt 9:9f], to Peter after he had denied the Lord three times [Jn 18:17, etc.], to the paralytic [Jn 5:5f] to whom, after the Lord had healed him, He said: "See, you are well! Sin no more, that nothing worse may befall you" [Jn 5:14]. By saying this He showed that the man had been taken by illness because of his sins and that, in being freed from the former, he had also received forgiveness of the latter, not because he had been praying for

it for a long time, nor because of fasting, nor due to his lying on the ground, but instead and only because of his conversion and unhesitating faith, his breaking-off with evil and true repentance and many tears, just as the harlot [Lk 7:38 and 44] and Peter who wept bitterly [Mt 26:75].

Here is the source of that great gift which is proper uniquely to God and which the Lord alone possessed. Next, just as He was about to ascend into heaven, He bequeathed this great charism to His disciples in His stead. How did He imbue them with this dignity and authority? Let us find out the what, and the how much, and the when. The chosen eleven disciples were gathered together behind closed doors. He entered and stood in their midst and breathed on them, saying: "Receive the Holy Spirit, whosoever sins you forgive, they are forgiven them; if you retain the sins of any, they are retained" [Jn 20:22-23]. At that time He enjoined on them nothing about penances, since they were going to be taught [about such things] by the Holy Spirit.

The Hierarchy has been Corrupted and left only with the Authority to Celebrate the Sacraments

13. As we said, therefore, the holy Apostles summoned this authority in succession for those who were to hold their thrones. Not one of the rest of the believers ever conceived of presuming upon it. The Lord's disciples preserved with all exactitude the rightness of this authority. But, as we said, when time had gone by, the worthy grew mixed and mingled with the unworthy, with one contending in order to have precedence over another and feigning virtue for the sake of preferment. Thus, because those who were holding the Apostles' thrones were shown up as fleshly minded, as lovers of pleasure and seekers of glory, and as inclining towards heresies, the divine grace abandoned them and this authority was taken away from them. Therefore, having abandoned as well everything else which is required of those who celebrate the sacraments, this

alone is demanded of them: that they be Orthodox. But I do not myself think that they are even this. Someone is not Orthodox just because he does not slip some new dogma into the Church of God, but because he possesses a life which keeps harmony with true teaching. Such a life and such a man contemporary patriarchs and metropolitans have at different times either looked for and not found, or, if they find him, they prefer [to ordain] the unworthy candidate instead. They ask only this of him, that he put the symbol of the faith [the Creed] down in writing. They find this alone acceptable, that the man be neither a zealot for the sake of what is good, nor that he do battle with anyone because of evil. In this way they pretend that they keep peace here in the Church. This is worse than active hostility [to God], and it is a cause of great unrest.

It is because of this that the priests have also grown worthless and no better than the people. None of them are that salt of which the Lord spoke [Mt 5:13], able to constrain and reprove and keep the life of another from wasting away. Instead, they are aware of and conceal each other's faults, and have become themselves inferior to the people, and the people in turn still worse than before. Some of the latter, though, have been revealed as superior to the priests. In the lightless gloom of the clergy these people appear as burning coals. If the former were, according to the Lord's word [Mt 5:16], to shine in their lives like the sun, then these coals would seem radiant but would be dark in comparison to the greater light. But, since only the likeness and the vesture of the priesthood is left among men, the gift of the Spirit has passed to the monks. It has been revealed through signs that they have entered by their actions into the life of the Apostles. Here too, however, the devil has been busy at his proper work. For when he saw that they had been revealed as, in a way, the new disciples of Christ in the world, and that they had shown forth in their lives and done miracles, he introduced false brethren, his disciples, and when, after a little while, these had multiplied (as you can see for yourself!), the monks as well were rendered useless and became altogether as if they were not monks at all.

Therefore, it is neither to those in the habit of monks, nor to those ordained and enrolled in the rank of the priesthood, nor yet to those who have been honored with the dignity of the episcopate—I mean the patriarchs and metropolitans and bishops—that God has given the grace of forgiving sins merely by virtue of their having been ordained. Perish the thought! For these are allowed only to celebrate the sacraments (and I think myself that even this does not apply to many of them, lest they be burned up entirely by this service who are themselves but straw). Rather, this grace is given alone to those, as many as there are among priests and bishops and monks, who have been numbered with Christ's disciples on account of their purity of life.

Signs of the True Intercessor: Apostolic Virtues and Boldness

14. How do such people become aware that they are enrolled among those whom I have spoken of, and how precisely will the others who are seeking them recognize them? The Lord Himself taught us the reply when He said: "And these signs will accompany those who believe: in My name they will cast out demons; they will speak in new tongues"—the latter means the God-inspired and edifying teaching of the word—"they will pick up serpents, and if they drink any deadly thing, it will not hurt them" [Mk 16:17-18]. He says elsewhere: "My sheep hear My voice" [Jn 10:27]; and again: "You will know them by their fruits" [Mt 7:16]. What are these fruits? Paul lists the majority of them when he says: "But the fruit of the Spirit is love, joy, peace, patience, kindness, faith, gentleness, self-control" [Gal 5:22], and to these we add compassion, brotherly love, alms-giving and everything which

follows from them. In addition there are:

> A word of wisdom, a word of knowledge, gifts of heal-
> ing and a multitude of other things, all of which are
> worked by one and the same Spirit, Who apportions to
> each one individually as He wills [see I Cor 12:8-11].

Those who have entered into participation of these virtues, whether in whole or in part, according to what is profitable to each, have been enlisted in the choir of the Apostles, and as many as accomplish them even today are also enrolled there. These people are therefore the "light of the world," as Christ Himself says: "No one lights a lamp and puts it under a bushel or beneath his bed, but on a stand so that it gives light to all in the house" [Mt 5:14-15]. Such people are recognized not just by these charisms, but by their manner of life as well. It is precisely thus that those who seek them out will recognize them, and each one of them himself, since they, as it were in the likeness of our Lord Jesus Christ, not only think it not shameful, but rather reckon humility and wretchedness the highest honor and, just as Christ, give proof of unfeigned obedience to their own fathers and guides while still subject to them. They are recognized in that they have loved dishonors and insults, curses and mockeries with all their soul, and have received those who laid these things upon them as providers of great blessings, and have prayed for them from the bottom of their heart and with tears. They are recognized if they have spat upon all the world's glory and have considered everything in it as trash. So why prolong the discourse by stating so much that is obvious? If, on the one hand, someone finds that he has attained every virtue which is set out in the holy scriptures, and if, on the other, he has pursued at the same time every practice of the good, and at every stage has experienced progress, alteration, and attainment, and if he has been borne aloft to the divine glory, *then* indeed may someone recognize himself as having become a participant of God and of His charismata, and so will he be known by as many as can see clearly, or even by those whose vision is less acute. Thus may such men speak to everyone approaching them with freedom of speech: "We are ambassadors for Christ, God making His appeal through us, be reconciled to God" [2 Cor 5:20].

All such men have kept God's commandments unto death. They have sold their belongings and distributed them among the poor. They have followed Christ by enduring temptations. They have lost their own lives in the world for the sake of their love for God, and have found them again unto life everlasting. And, when they discovered again their own souls, they found within themselves an intelligible light and thus, in this light, they saw the light unapproachable, God Himself, according to what is written: "In Your light we shall see light" [Ps 36:9]. How is it possible to see anything which is proper to the soul? Pay attention! The soul of each is that drachma which—not God, but—each of us lost [Lk 15:8ff] when we sank into the darkness of sin. But Christ, the true light, when He had come and met with those who seek Him, in a way that He alone knows, gave them grace to see Himself. This is what it means to find one's own soul: to see God, and in His light to become oneself higher than all the visible creation, and to have Him inside oneself as shepherd and teacher. From Him as well, this person will also know how, if you like, to bind and loose, and, as knowing truly, will worship the One Who gave him this grace and will provide it in turn to those who need.

Symeon's Personal Witness to His own Elder

15. I know, my child, that the authority to bind and loose is given to such people by God the Father and our Lord Jesus Christ through the Holy Spirit, to those who are sons by adoption and His holy servants. I was myself a discile to such a father, one who did not have the ordination from men, but who brought me by the hand—or better, by the spirit—into

discipleship, and who commanded me, who for a long time had been moved by the Holy Spirit to a great longing for it, to receive the ordination from men according to the traditional order.

16. Therefore, brothers and fathers, let us pray first of all to become such men as these, and only then let us talk to others about the deliverance from passions and endurance of evil thoughts. Let us seek out such a spiritual father. Indeed, let us put every effort into finding such men, the true disciples of Christ, and let us beseech God with an aching heart and many tears for literally days on end that He may unveil the eyes of our hearts in order for us to recognize them (if indeed such a one is to be found anywhere in this evil generation) so that, on finding one, we may receive forgiveness of our sins through him, obeying his ordinances and commandments with all our soul, just as he, having heard those of Christ, became a participant of His grace and gifts, and, aflame with the Holy Spirit, received from Christ the authority to bind and to loose, to which Holy Spirit is due all glory, honor and worship, together with the Father and the Only-Begotten Son, forever. Amen.

Bibliography

1. Works of St. Symeon and Their Abbreviations

AK   *Symeon Neos Theologos: HYMNEN (Kritischer Text, Indices, Prolegomena besorgt von Athanasios Kambylis). Berlin/New York: Walter de Gruyter, 1976.*

C   *Catéchèses* (Introduction, texte critique et notes par B. Krivocheine, traduction par J. Paramelle). *SC* 96, 104, and 113 (1963, 1964, and 1965).

deC   *Symeon the New Theologian: The Discourses* (trans. C.J. deCantanzaro; introduction by G. Maloney). New York: Paulist Press, 1980.

Ch   *Chapitres Théologiques, Gnostiques, et Pratiques* (Introduction, texte critique, et notes par J. Darrouzes). *SC* 51 (1957).

McG   *Symeon the New Theologian: the Practical and Theological Chapters and the Three Theological Discourses* (trans. and introduction by P. McGuckin). Kalamazoo, Michigan: Cistercian Studies, 1982.

ED   *Traités théologiques et éthiques* (Introduction, texte critique, traduction et notes par Jean Darrouzès). *SC* 122 and 129 (1966, 1967).

H   *Syméon le nouveau théologien: Hymnes.* No's. 1-15 (Introduction, texte critique, et notes par J. Koder, traduction par J. Paramelle). *SC* 156 (1969). No's. 16-40 (Texte critique par J. Koder, traduction et notes par L. Neyrand). *SC* 174 (1971). No's. 41-58 (Texte critique par J. Koder, traduction et notes par L. Neyrand et J. Paramelle). *SC* 196 (1973).

M   *Hymns of Divine Love* (trans. G. A. Maloney). Denville,
         New Jersey: Dimension Books, n.d.

2. Other Abbreviations used in Introduction and Notes

ACW   *Ancient Christian Writers*

ANF   *Ante-Nicene Fathers*

DOP   *Dumbarton Oaks Papers*

ECR   *Eastern Churches Review*

GCS   *Die griechische christlichen Schriftsteller der ersten drei
         Jahrhunderten*

GOTR   *Greek Orthodox Theologian Review*

JTS   *Journal of Theological Studies*

Ir.   *Irénikon*

NPNF   *Nicene, Post-Nicene Fathers*

OCP   *Orientalia Christiana Periodica*

PG   *Patrologia Graeca*

PL   *Patrologia Latina*

PO   *Patrologia Orientalia*

SC   *Sources chrétiennes*

SP   *Studia Patristica*

SVTQ   *St. Vladimir's Theological Quarterly*

3. Secondary Works
(limited to studies of Symeon himself, or of his immediate period)

Biedermann, H.M. *Das Menschenbild bei Symeon dem Jungeren,
    dem Theologen*. Würzburg: 1949.

Browning, R. "Church, State and Learning in Twelfth-Century Byzantium." *Friends of Dr. William's Library*, 34th Lecture (1980). London: Valiorum rep., 1989, 5-24.

Charamis, P. "The Monk as an Element of Byzantine Society." *DOP* 25 (1971): 63-84.

Christophorides, V.C. *He pneumatike patrotes kata Symeon ton neon Theologon.* Thessalonica: 1977.

Fraigneau-Julien, B. *Les sens spirituels et la vision de Dieu selon Syméon le nouveau théologien. Théologie historique* 67. Paris: 1985.

Golitzin, A., "Hierarchy vs Anarchy? Dionysius Areopagita, Symeon the New Theologian, Nicetas Stethatos and their Common Roots in Ascetical Tradition," SVTQ 38.2 (1994), 131-179.

Gouillard, J. "Constantine Chyrsomallos sous le masque de Syméon le nouveau théologien." Travaux et Mémoires V (1973): 313-327.

_____. "Quatre procès de mystique à Byzance (vers 960-1143)." *Révue des études byzantines* 36 (1978): 5-81.

Graef, H. "The Spiritual Director in the Thought of Symeon the New Theologian." In *Kyriakon: Festschrift Johannes Quasten*, vol. II. Edited by P. Cranfield and J.A. Jungmann. Münster: 1970, 608-614.

Hackel, S., editor. *The Byzantine Saint. Studies Supplementary to Sobornost* 5. London: 1981.

Hatzopoulos, A., *Two Outstanding Cases in Byzantine Spirituality: the Macarian Homilies and Symeon the New Theologian* (Thessalonica, 1991).

Holl, K., *Enthusiasmus und Bußgewalt beim griechischen Mönchtum: eine Studie zum Symeon dem neuen Theologen* (Leipzig, 1898).

Hussey, J.M. *Ascetics and Humanists in XIth-century Byzantium.* London: 1960.

_____. *Church and Learning in the Byzantine Empire: 867-1185.* London: 1960.

_____. "Symeon and Nicholas Cabasilas: Similarities and Contrasts in Orthodox Spirituality." *ECR* IV,2 (1972): 131-140.

Krivocheine, B. "Essence créée et essence divine dans la théologie spirituelle de S. Syméon le nouveau théologien." *Messager de l'exarchat du Patriarche Russe en Europe Occidentale* 75/76: 151-170.

_____. "*Ho anhyperephanos theos.* St. Symeon the New Theologian and early Christian popular Piety. *SP* 2 (1957): 485-494.

_____. *In the Light of Christ: St. Symeon the New Theologian: Life, Spirituality, Doctrine.* Translated by Anthony P. Gythiel. Crestwood, New York: 1986.

_____. "Le thème de l'ivresse spirituelle dans la mystique de saint Syméon le nouveau théologien." *SP* 5 (1962): 368-376.

_____. "Saint Syméon le nouveau théologien et Nicetas Stéthatos: histoire du texte des Catéchèses." *Akten des XI internationalen Byzantinisten-Kongresses.* München: 1960.

_____. "The Writings of St. Symeon the New Theologian." *OCP* 20 (1954): 298-328.

Lanne, E. "L'interprétation palamite de la vision de Saint Benoît." In *Le Millenaire du Mont Athos: 963-1963,* vol. II. Venezia: 1963, 21-47.

Loos, M. *Dualist Heresy in the Middle Ages.* Prague: 1972.

Macrides, R. "Saints and Sainthood in the early Paleologan Period." In *The Byzantine Saint.* London: 1981, 67-87.

Magdalinos, P. "The Byzantine Holy Man in the Twelfth Century." In *The Byzantine Saint.* London: 1981, 51-66.

Maloney, G.A. *The Mystic of Fire and Light: St. Symeon the New Theologian.* Danville, N.J.: 1975.

Mary, S.S. "St. Symeon the New Theologian and the Way of Tears." *SP* 7 (1966): 355-361.

Miguel, P. "La conscience de la grâce selon Syméon le nouveau théologien." *Ir.* XLII, 3 (1969): 314-342.

_____. "*Peira*: contribution à l'étude du vocabulaire de l'expérience religieuse dans l'oeuvre de Maxime le Confesseur." *SP* 7 (1966): 355-361.

Morris, R. "The Political Saint of the Eleventh Century." In *The Byzantine Saint*. London: 1981, 43-50.

Nicol, D.M. *Church and Society in the Last Centuries of Byzantium*. Cambridge: 1979.

Patlagean, E. "Sainteté et pouvoir." In *The Byzantine Saint*. London: 1981, 88-105.

Rosenthal-Kamarinea, I. "Symeon Studites, ein heiliger Narr." *Akten des XI internationale Byzantinisten-Kongresses*. München: 1960, 515-520.

van Rossum, J. "Priesthood and Confession in St. Symeon the New Theologian." *SVTQ* 20 (1976): 220-228.

_____. "Reflections on Byzantine Ecclesiology: Nicetas Stethatos' 'On the Hierarchy.'" *SVTQ* 25 (1981): 75-83.

Ryden, L. "The Holy Fool." In *The Byzantine Saint*. London: 1981, 106-113.

Soteropoulos, H.G. *Neptikoi Pateres 1: Symeon ho neos theologos (Bios, Erga, Didaskalia)*. Athenai: 1986.

Stathopoulos, D.L. "Die Gottesliebe (*theios eros*) bei Symeon dem neuen Theologen." Dissertation. Bonn: 1964.

_____. "The Divine Light in the Poetry of St. Symeon the New Theologian." *GOTR* 19,2 (1974): 95-111.

Turner, H.J.M. "St. Symeon the New Theologian and Dualist Heresies—Comparisons and Contrasts." *SVTQ* 32,4 (1988): 359-366.

_____. *St. Symeon the New Theologian and Spiritual Fatherhood*. Leiden: 1990.

Völker, W. *Praxis und theoria bei Symeon dem neuen Theologen: ein Beitrag zur Byzantinischen Mystik*. Wiesbaden: 1974.

Ware, K.T. "Forward," to Irenee Hausherr's *Spiritual Direction in the Early Christian East*. Cistercian Studies 116. Kalamazoo: 1990, vii-xxxiii.

_____. "The Mystery of God and Man in St. Symeon the New Theologian." *Sobornost* 6,4 (1972): 227-236.

_____. "The Spiritual Father in Orthodox Christianity." *Cross Currents* XXIV (1974): 296-313.

Index of Scriptural References

Index

T

POPULAR PATRISTICS SERIES

ST VLADIMIR'S SEMINARY PRESS
1-800-204-2665 • www.svspress.com